The Show Border Collie

JOYCE COLLIS

RINGPRESS BOOKS

To Felix Cosme who made history in the breed piloting his adored Tilehouse Cassius at Beagold to become the first show champion and the first border collie to compete in the Contest of Champions.

Acknowledgements

Many thanks to all the people who have contributed photographs of their dogs and to Felix Cosme for his help compiling all the facts and figures

RINGPRESS

Ringpress Books
an imprint of Ringpress Ltd.,
Spirella House, Letchworth, Herts SG6 4ET

Text © Joyce Collis and Ringpress Ltd., 1988

First published 1988

ISBN No. 0948955 35X

Production Consultants Landmark Ltd.
Typeset by DP Photosetting, Aylesbury, Bucks
Printed and bound in Great Britain
by The Bath Press

Contents

Foreword

AS an ex chairman and long standing committee member of the Border Collie Club of Great Britain and owner of one of the first show champions and the breed's top stud dog – Show Champion Tork of Whenway – it gives me great pleasure to write this foreword for the first book dealing solely with the border collie as a show breed.

There is no other breed of dog which within so short a space of time has become so popular as a show dog as the border collie. Entries at championship shows continue to increase and are fast approaching the two hundred mark. Renowned for its working ability with sheep and cattle and also in obedience, agility competitions and working trials it is now also regarded as a firmly established 'show breed', more and more people involved in other breeds are discovering the charm, intelligence and faithfulness of this wonderful breed.

Joyce Collis the authoress is a championship show judge of many breeds and awards challenge certificates in border collies, bearded collies and smooth collies. As well as judging in many countries of the world she was the first breed specialist judge to officiate at Crufts Dog Show in the border collie ring. She is also a successful breeder and exhibitor and together with Mr Felix Cosme was the owner of the first border collie show champion – 'Tilehouse Cassius at Beagold'.

Novices and the regular exhibitor alike can rest assured that they are receiving sound expert advice and the novice exhibitor or budding showgoer who studies this book and follows the advice given will avoid making the mistakes which are so disheartening and costly both in time and money.

Finally let me take this opportunity to wish this book the success that it richly deserves.

BRUCE KILSBY

Preface

THE shelves are crowded with books on the working sheepdog, the border collie competing and training for sheep trials and obedience successes. At the beginning my partner Felix Cosme and I tried to join this dedicated band of enthusiasts, but without success. To be honest, we knew we would be out of our depth competing with such experts in a completely different way of life, so we were not so very sorry when we did not succeed.

We had for years been dedicated show exhibitors, this is the life we enjoyed and understood so our border collies would be for the show ring. This book is purely and simply about the show border collie. I have not attempted to write about the breed's history, nor its capabilities as a sheep trial competitor and I certainly would not encroach on the obedience side of this versatile breed.

Commonsense must prevail before chosing a border collie for show or as a companion. This super intelligent animal has been bred for generations to work and live an active life, so it is vital that regular training is given daily. The border collie must not be allowed to become bored with its life and consequently get into mischief. Unless it is trained to behave and suppress its natural liveliness on certain occasions, it cannot be expected to act like breeds that have been exhibited in the show ring for many years. With proper treatment the reward will be boundless – an adoring, keen to please, intelligent companion for life.

Joyce Collis
September 1988

CHAPTER ONE

The Show Border Collie Arrives

THERE was a great flurry of opposition from many quarters when it became widely known that the border collie was to be accepted by the Kennel Club as a show dog. The Border Collie Club of Great Britain held its inaugural meeting in 1975 and set about forming a Breed Standard. This, together with a request for recognition, was sent to the Kennel Club. It was not until June 1976 that the Kennel Club gave their permission, and the following was published in the Kennel Gazette:

'The General Committee of the Kennel Club has decided that the border collie shall be recognised as a breed for show purposes in accordance with conditions set out below. This decision was reached after full and lengthy discussion with the International Sheepdog Society, whose co-operation has been sought. For some time there have been requests from border collie enthusiasts that the breed be recognised for show purposes. The Kennel Club has hitherto withheld such recognition on the grounds that although there exists a recognised type, there was insufficient evidence of reliable true-to-type breeding.

'It is now evident that more attention has been given to developing the border collies as a true breed from the physical as distinct from the purely working point of view. The International Sheepdog Society is interested only in the working ability of the border collie; it does not lay down a standard for the breed, nor does it wish to do so. It has its own registration system and its own sphere of activity (sheep trials) which will not be affected by the Kennel Club recognition of the breed. Should any owners of Kennel Club registered border collies wish their dogs to compete in International Sheep Dog Society controlled activities, they will necessarily have to effect appropriate membership registration with the ISDS. Registration with the Kennel Club will not suffice. It should be noted the ISDS will only accept a dog for registration if both parents are ISDS registered or it is proved an outstanding working dog.'

This notification explained in full the formalities needed for the transition of ISDS registered border collies on to the register of the Kennel Club.

Unfortunately, misunderstanding and frustration occurred when owners decided that they wanted to show their dogs, and found to their dismay that either the sire or dam of their border collie did not have the necessary papers. They were therefore ineligable to register their dogs for exhibition with the Kennel Club's permission.

The Kennel Club issued a directive for the conditions for Kennel Club Registration of border collies.

'Registration of border collies will be permitted only of dogs already themselves registered with the ISDS, or of dogs whose parents are registered either with the ISDS or the Kennel Club. This procedure has always been followed for the acceptance of border collies in the Kennel Club working trials and obedience record.

'The ISDS registration of ancestors must be quoted when applying for the Kennel Club registration unless the parents are already KC registered. The ISDS has undertaken to provide relevant authentication, if necessary. In the absence of such evidence, a border collie will not be accepted in the KC register. If one or both parents are not registered with the ISDS or the KC, the dog may only be entered in working trials and obedience register. Application for registration of border collies with the KC may be made from

▼ *Frank Garwood.*

Crufts 1982: Catherine Sutton awarded the first challenge certificates to Tilehouse Cassius at Beagold (left) and Tracelyn Gal.

August 1, 1976.'

The directive goes on to give information about the necessary forms needed to comply with their wishes. But as so often happens, entirely new forms are issued and the information is then soon out of date. It is always wisest to contact the Kennel Club themselves when the need arises and then you can be certain of getting the correct forms.

An enormous amount of work was done by dedicated border collie owners to iron out the problems that arose. Considerable tact and understanding was needed to satisfy both sides and eventually a workable compromise was established, with credit going to both the International Sheepdog Society and the Kennel Club.

The late Major Glover was involved with bringing the border collie into the show ring and was quite rightly proud of the part he played in the breed's recognition. The stage was set for him to have the honour of being the first ever judge to award challenge certificates to the border collies in 1982 at Crufts Championship Show. But sadly the huge entry waited in vain for Major Glover was too ill to officiate. He died later that year. The honour of giving the Crufts 1982 challenge certificates passed to Mrs Catherine Sutton, and history was made in the breed when Felix Cosme received the first challenge certificate and best of breed with Tilehouse Cassius at Beagold. The first bitch challenge certificate went to Eric Broadhurst's Tracelyn Gal. The show border collie had arrived and the popularity of this handsome and versatile breed has grown from that moment onwards.

Long coated border collie types.

Typical working sheepdogs pictured at about 1915 showing simalarities to both the bearded collie and border collie.

CHAPTER TWO

The Beagold Border Collies

MY interest has always been in the working and hunting breed of dog. As a child I spent hours in a fox hound kennels in India getting in the way, but all the time soaking up the atmosphere and enjoying every minute of the day with the hounds. Many years later when we returned to England I followed the beagle pack in Devon and could not wait to own my first beagle.

The beagles adjusted well to being shown, even though they spent the weekends working. My dogs' show careers were regularly intermingled with hunting. Never once did they catch the hare, but many times it was sighted. The joy of the chase has never left my memory. Then, the following week, bathed and groomed they would be competing at a championship show. The dogs and bitches were quite happy to subdue their natural instincts, walk sedately across the show ring and then stand still for inspection by the judge.

The breed was not ruined because it was being shown, the temperament was not drastically altered. This, I think is significant for those border collie enthusiasts who fear the effect that showing might have on what is first and foremost, a working breed. The fact is that it has all happened before without dire results. Beagles are still being shown, and meetings are still held regularly for the dogs to hunt the hare.

My first sight of the border collie at work was in Scotland in 1962. We visited several farms and talked to the farmers about their dogs. Many of the collies in that area were long coated, and must have had quite strong lines to the bearded collie, which was used more as a cattle dog but also worked on farms with sheep. The first bearded collies were brought in for recognition by the Kennel Club in 1949. There must have been many out-crosses to the border collie, all descending from the original working sheepdog. We returned to watch the border collies at work for several days. They worked alone, ushering their charges through hilly countryside, along minute tracks, across rocky outcrops, as if they had suckers on their paws. Never wavering, working with a purpose and with unmistakable joy. Even from that distance, we could appreciate their expertise and tremendous concentration.

On closer inspection we found marked similarities in the character and

To this day, would be owners still ask for Welsh border collies. This is an early tri-colour border collie from the Welsh area.

Sheepdogs at work.

make up of the border collie and the bearded collie. It was quite evident that they had descended from the same ancestors. Even to this day one or two of the bearded collie lines can produce smooth coated bearded collies, with unmistakable resemblances to the border. At that time, the border collie was not recognised for show by the Kennel Club, and as we were dedicated show people we had to choose the working descendant of the sheepdog in the form of the bearded collie. In that early stage we found they had similar temperaments, and that degree of wildness only found in the working unspoilt breeds.

Starting off with the bearded collie helped us to understand and enjoy the stronger character and similar requirements of the border collie which we purchased as soon as they were recognised for show by the Kennel Club. In 1963 the show bearded collie was pretty wild and just as active in the show ring. The number of bearded collie owners and breeders was very few, in fact the breed had almost become extinct. The herdsmen and shepherds had many unregistered working dogs, but as they were not registered with any particular society, they were difficult to trace. Several types of long coated bearded collies had been brought from Scotland and the North of England with very little knowledge of their ancestors, so it is quite feasible that borders and beardies have been crossed several times.

In fact, at that early stage in the beardies' development the Kennel Club allowed unregistered bearded collie types to be brought into the breeding programme so that the breed could get established. The resulting litters were given a Class II registration and could not be exported. After three generations of breeding to registered dogs it was hoped that they would breed true, and the KC gave their permission for the progeny to be exported.

The situation when the border collie was recognised for show by the KC was entirely different. Using the International Sheepdog Society Register, show enthusiasts could pick and chose from many established lines. Those gifted with an eye for a good quality, well constructed farm bred border collie, started the foundation of many winning show dogs. There was always the hope that one or two in each litter would be suitable for show. There is no reason why such an intelligent breed as the border collie should not take to the show ring, with as much enjoyment and capability for winning as the beardie.

The bearded collie is given the full title of champion when it wins the necessary three challenge certificates. There is very little chance of the dogs being allowed to work as their ancestors did, so the breed clubs have devised working tests which are a mixture of obedience, agility and trials. These tests are optional and have become very popular, with both dogs and owners enjoying the competition. The border collie has not been given this option

A border collie pup at two weeks.

A two and a half week old bearded collie puppy. It has similar markings to the border collie and is also the same length and general shape. The only noticeable difference is the border collie's ears which are higher set and smaller.

they are considered only as show champions when they win the three challenge certificates in the show ring under three different judges. Then they must then take the tests working with sheep and pass with an agreed score, before they can become full champions.

There is very little opportunity for border collie owners to work their dogs with sheep. In fact, several experienced border collie owners have mentioned that the border collie used only once or twice to work sheep could become frustrated and difficult to cope with, so it would be best if they were not introduced to the task. So at the moment the border collie is confined to show champion status.

It was in 1976, after my partner Felix Cosme had joined the Beagold Kennels that we decided to include the border collie in our family. By that time they had been recognised for show by the Kennel Club, and we set about searching for suitable stock. It was no easy task for the fear that the show border collie would be altered and would not have the brains to work had caused considerable animosity and controversy. The antis said that the breed would be split in two – maybe three – when including the obedience trained dogs. They failed to see that border collies bred soley for show would not affect the trial or farm dogs. Obedience competitors have done wonders with their border collies for many years and that has not affected the trial competitors or the farmers. In fact, many borders bred on farms for sheep working did not match up to the requirements. Not all borders are capable of work, so they found their way to people's homes as pets and to obedience breeders, long before the show people went searching for stock. Personally, I feel that the acceptance of the breed in the show ring will help to take in many of those surplus good looking borders, with the capability to work, but not the inclination.

After much consideration we decided to buy our foundation stock straight from the farm, although we had seen some very good borders in the obedience ring. For two years we planned and searched for the show type that we wanted, but with very little success. We thought if we could meet the people who had been working their borders over the years and talk to them, we could convince them that we wanted the breed to show, but we had every intention of training them regularly and would welcome any help or advice they could offer.

Our first successful visit was to a sheep farmer in Northampton. He did not welcome us with open arms, but he did offer help and advice. He was also willing to let us see Lad, the sire of the litter he had in the barn, work the large flock of sheep in the nearby field. Lad was a handsome black dog and had complete control, it was obvious he was a super worker. Farmer Nunnely then took us to see the litter of seven week old puppies. They were running around showing no signs of nervousness. While the farmer praised the working capabilities of their parents, I was busy assessing the show potential of each puppy. There was one I liked very much. She was a well shaped little bitch with a nice head, a friendly out going character and no signs of nervousness when I picked her up. We both agreed that this one would grow into a good looking black and white show puppy.

Then Mr Nunnely stepped on the pup. Of course, from then on she hid in the corner of the barn and no amount of encouragement could get the poor little mite out. Reluctantly, we decided to leave the pups and try elsewhere. On the way back to the car we saw two older pups in the nearby pig sty. Mr Nunnely explained that his friend had used Lad and these two puppies had not yet been sold. The dog puppy was nice, about three months old. The bitch had an excellent shape and a sweet feminine head, without being too fine. When she moved, she glided over the ground. I realised immediately that she answered all my requirements. Her show potential was evident. So that is how Destiny of Beagold became our first border collie.

She was extremely lively from the start, but not so different from the early bearded collies. But we discovered that a border collie trait was to mouth the muzzle of another dog. Of course, there is no 'beard' to be pulled off in other border collies but the beardie bitch Destiny was running with soon lost all signs of her whiskers and beard. We therefore had to kennel Destiny on her own, especially when we were not about. The size of the runs and kennels that we had for each dog was suitable and more than adequate for the border. Destiny exercised herself, digging and devouring every blade of grass that had grown in the compound and in next to no time her run was a sea of mud and large holes. She liked it that way.

We took Destiny on a thirteen mile sponsored walk in aid of the Border Collie Rescue, we were certain that this would tire her out. Making our way across the fields, she was good and we had no trouble until we got to the route following a busy road. Then she tried to work every car that passed by. We had trained her to drop on command when a car passed while on our daily walks, then when the car had gone by she would resume walking to heel. But on this sponsored walk, on a Sunday afternoon the traffic was nose to tail. As every one of the cars passed Destiny dropped to the ground and refused to move until it had gone by. Needless to say, we were left far behind. Late that night in the dark we finally finished our walk, exhausted, frustrated and threatening never to take her near another road.

We then began our search for a suitable stud dog. We had studied and admired Mrs Barbara Carpenter's breeding. Her Brocken border collies looked like winners in every field of activity. We also wanted a calmer temperament. Destiny needed a slightly more sociable and not so wild

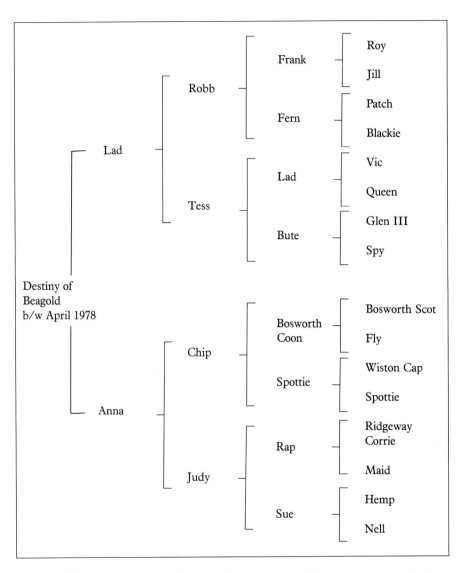

Destiny of
Beagold
b/w April 1978

Lad
— Robb
— — Frank
— — — Roy
— — — Jill
— — Fern
— — — Patch
— — — Blackie
— Tess
— — Lad
— — — Vic
— — — Queen
— — Bute
— — — Glen III
— — — Spy

Anna
— Chip
— — Bosworth Coon
— — — Bosworth Scot
— — — Fly
— — Spottie
— — — Wiston Cap
— — — Spottie
— Judy
— — Rap
— — — Ridgeway Corrie
— — — Maid
— — Sue
— — — Hemp
— — — Nell

partner. We were told that Mrs Iris Combe of the Tilehouse Border Collies was the owner of Brocken Sweep and she intended to mate her bitch Fly of Tilehouse to Sweep. He was a handsome nicely made tri-colour dog. Fly was black and white.

   We contacted Mrs Combe and reserved a puppy dog from that litter. We also learnt that Sweep was in-bred on Brocken Robbie, a dog whose reputation was well known as a good producer. Dr Sheila Grew, editor of the Working Sheepdog News, wrote about him in glowing terms: 'He is well known for his breeding potential, passing on the finest herding qualities of

Felix Cosme with Show Champion Tilehouse Cassius at Beagold.

the great legendary dogs of the past, these same qualities continuing in his descendants and the most successful present day lines. He was a strong heavy boned rough coated black and tan dog. Intelligent and sensitive of a gentle happy temperament'.

It was not surprising that we wanted to own Brocken foundation stock. We brought home our dog puppy when he was five weeks old. The breeder was very pleased with the litter and pointed out our puppy, remarking on how strong and healthy he was. He had come into the world fighting and had taken up the best place at his mother's teat. This handsome little pup was to be a birthday present for my partner and as he is an ardent boxing fan, he named him Cassius. Little did we know that this little pup would follow his namesake and make history.

Seven months later we heard that Barbara Carpenter was willing to part with Brocken Sweep's little brother Moss. Moss was the despair of the Carpenter household. From such illustrious parents and with ancestors who were champions, he did not want to work with sheep. He was like Ferdinand the bull, who had been bred to fight in the bullring in Spain, but prefered to sit all day in the sun and smell the flowers. Moss saw no reason why he should move the sheep from one field to another. Commands, shouts and

Brocken Moss of Beagold stealing the rice pudding.

directions just went over his head, he just did not want to know. He was a good looking tri-colour dog, and Barbara thought he might be good enough to show.

"That is all he is good for," she said with disgust. We went to stay for the weekend at her beautiful farm in Bream. The snow was covering the ground making the beautiful Gloucestershire countryside even more picturesque. We met all her borders and were pleased to accept Moss. She waved us goodbye with tears in her eyes. She did not want to part with Moss but with many other excellent workers to feed, he was just a passenger on a busy farm.

By now we were really captivated by the breed. Their intelligence and loving character was all that we could wish for in a dog. Bonnie of Beagold was the next bitch we bought from Ray Edwards, a shepherd who also regularly worked his dogs in the trials. Bonnie was black and white, a beautifully shaped puppy. In fact, she was better in construction than Destiny. Destiny had a light brown eye, Bonnie's eyes were very dark brown, which is probably the reason why she won more show prizes in the ring.

It was a very exciting day when Joe Kat from Holland came to judge the breed in Wales. He had bred border collies for many years and knew exactly what he wanted. He explained to the exhibitors in each class how he wanted

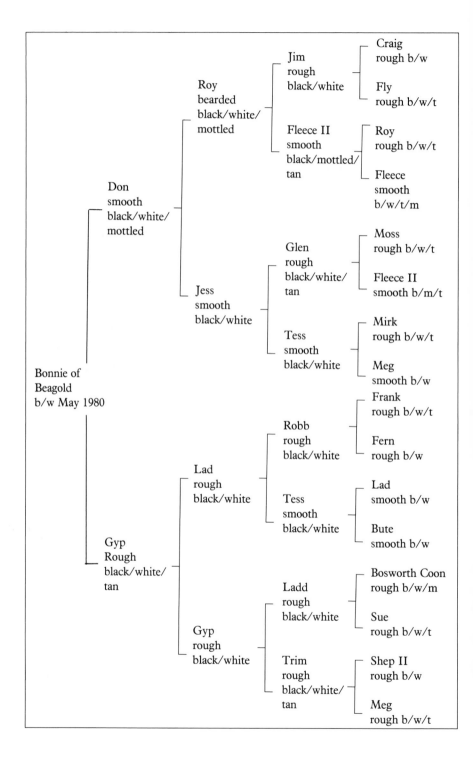

Bonnie of
Beagold
b/w May 1980

Don
smooth
black/white/
mottled

Gyp
Rough
black/white/
tan

Roy
bearded
black/white/
mottled

Jess
smooth
black/white

Lad
rough
black/white

Gyp
rough
black/white

Jim
rough
black/white

Fleece II
smooth
black/mottled/
tan

Glen
rough
black/white/
tan

Tess
smooth
black/white

Robb
rough
black/white

Tess
smooth
black/white

Ladd
rough
black/white

Trim
rough
black/white/
tan

Craig
rough b/w

Fly
rough b/w/t

Roy
rough b/w/t

Fleece
smooth
b/w/t/m

Moss
rough b/w/t

Fleece II
smooth b/m/t

Mirk
rough b/w/t

Meg
smooth b/w

Frank
rough b/w/t

Fern
rough b/w

Lad
smooth b/w

Bute
smooth b/w

Bosworth Coon
rough b/w/m

Sue
rough b/w/t

Shep II
rough b/w

Meg
rough b/w/t

Bonnie of Beagold.
Dam of Show Champion
Beagold Louis.

their dogs shown, emphasising that they should be on a loose lead. We had trained Bonnie and Cassius to move as they should and we were delighted to win best bitch with Bonnie and best of breed with Cassius. Then Cassius was taken into the enormous working group ring, and to very loud applause was placed reserve in the group by judge Douglas Appleton who was very familiar with the breed. This was the first time that a border collie had been placed so high in the working group.

Our foundation bitches Bonnie and Destiny were bred along similar lines. Our foundation dogs Moss and Cassius were line bred on Brocken Robbie. From this combination we hoped to produce good looking border collies, with the capability to work but not the need. We intended to show their offspring so they had to comply with the standard drawn up by the Kennel Club. These lines were also in-bred with the capabilities for them to work on both sides, although it was doubtful that they would be called on to work, we certainly did not want to lose this characteristic. We also felt that the excellent temperament of both dogs should water down the liveliness of the bitch lines. Temperament is a major factor, as any well established breeder of show dogs is aware. A sharp temperament that might bite the judge or show aggression in the show ring is of no use whatsoever. From the litters

Askoa Cherokee at Firelynx: One of the earliest show border collies.

Show winners: Tri-coloured Beagold Sugar Ray sired by Cassius out of Bonnie of Beagold, handled by Felix Cosme Alpha Beesting finished runner-up.

planned, we hoped to find one or maybe two outstanding puppies of super quality, the real high flyers in the show ring.

The pedigrees of Bonnie and Destiny both show that they were bred completely from International Sheepdog Society working border collies. Now several years later it can be seen that the type of pedigrees have altered compared to the Kennel Club registered pedigrees like that of Beagold Hot Pepper (Show Champion Beagold Louis ex Fieldbank Virginia). As time passes there will be many other breeders who decide to simply register their show borders with the Kennel Club. This is because they are unlikely to have the opportunity to work their dogs, but will be keen regular exhibitors in the beauty show ring.

Soon after Bonnie was judged best bitch and Cassius won the reserve in the working group, we mated the pair. The resulting litter was small – just one dog and one bitch – but we were delighted with the strong, healthy pups. The dog Sugar Ray enjoyed considerable success in the show ring over here before being exported to Finland. He was a tri-colour and the Fins, who were new to the breed, wanted to establish tri-colour breeding lines. He has consequently proved to be a popular and successful sire.

Marc Henrie. ▼

Show Champion Beagold Louis.

Cassius's second litter to Bonnie produced five dogs and one bitch. We had planned to keep a black and white dog puppy from this litter so we had a nice variety to choose from. Beagold Louis was our choice, from the very beginning. He had all the good points from his sire and dam, perfectly marked, excellent construction and very outgoing in character. At one time we wondered if we had made the correct decision as the other dogs also matured into outstanding puppies. It was obvious that Cassius's and Bonnie's lines tied together well. We kept to our first choice Louis, who continued to improve as he matured. This confirmed our decision that he was definitely the pick of the litter. This combination did not produce any major faults and we were pleased to receive reports of the puppies and photographs from their new owners.

Next we mated Destiny to Cassius and we could see from the resulting litter that Cassius's line was the dominant one, producing his like in several of the progeny. Destiny was mated to Moss for her next litter. The resulting puppies were sound and good construction but they did not have the same good quality. Size was a problem in the dogs and although the pups' ears were small, they were not carried in the correct way. Destiny's ears were rather low set and she had passed this on to her offspring. Cassius was Moss's nephew, but it was obvious that Fly of Tilehouse was the dominant half of the parents of Cassius.

It was a fascinating situation, we were working completly in the dark when planning litters. The pedigrees of their ancestors gave no information on colour, type or construction. We could only learn by our mistakes and pick out from each litter the pup that would carry on the points we were looking for, never losing sight of the type that we had been attracted to in the first place.

We had kept a bitch from Cassius and Destiny and found that with all her good points, the one that we needed to correct was ear carriage. So we looked for a stud with strong ear carriage, held correctly with a slight tip. This we had seen in Show Champion Tork of Whenway who was owned by Bruce and Sheena Kilsby. He seemed the ideal partner for the bitch to double up on excellent construction, good movement, head and temperament, plus the added bonus of excellent ear carriage. From this litter we put all our hopes in Beagold Secret Ballot. Sadly she had everything we had hoped for, except high tipped ears. In fact, they were lower set than any of our previous litters.

In order to establish our own strain without too much in-breeding we needed to buy in another bitch. We started hunting round the show rings and eventually decided to bring in a bitch from Kathy Lister's Show Champion Fieldbank Professional. He was a tri-colour soundly built dog with excellent temperament who had been mated to Fieldbank Merrymeg. She was black

Fieldbank Merrymeg: dam of Fieldbank Virginia.

and white and like a true worker, she was never still. She was well made and of good temperament. The pair complimented each other and this was evident in the resulting litter. We were offered second pick of the pups and chose Fieldbank Virginia. She was a character that had retained all the good points from her sire and dam, plus the active working abilities obvious in Meg and the obedience capabilities from her sire's ancestors.

Virginia never did succeed in the show ring. She was beautifully constructed and a potential show bitch, but she refused to act like a show bitch. Her working instinct would never allow her to relax for a minute. In the show ring when the breeze blew leaves off the trees she plunged forward after them. A passing bird took her complete attention. Reluctantly, I let her go to a friend who kept sheep and cows and who needed help to bring the sheep into the home field at night.

I visited my friend a month later and learnt the true facts about Virginia. She would not leave the side of her new owner for a moment. The sheep and cows were of no interest to her at all. Sometimes she tried to work the old goat in the shed, but her first love was simply being with people. Virginia was mated to Louis and we kept a very nice black and white bitch from the litter, Beagold Hot Pepper.

With our foundation stock carefully chosen, we could now look to the future of our own strain. It is vital not to lose sight of the most important characteristics of the breed and good temperament is essential in any show dog. Several of our original dogs and bitches have died but their decendants are carbon copies with superb temperaments, proving that our lines are dominant. Although we prefer the black and white colour, we have fallen for a red and white bitch of excellent quality, Show Champion Passim's Bonnie at Beagold. This lovely bitch was the first to win enough points for a junior warrant, she was also the first red and white to win a challenge certificate and best of breed under specialist judge Mrs Barbara Beaumont. Her second challenge certificate was won under an all round judge Robin Searle and her third challenge certificate and title was also won under an all round judge, Ben Raven. With the first ever red and white bitch being made up to a show champion I am sure others will follow. We now intend to mate Bonnie. Whether we get red puppies in the litter is not so important, they will carry the genes for red when mated to a similar type of dog. It would certainly be nice to get a quality red and white dog and that is our ultimate aim.

CHAPTER THREE

The Standard

I HAVE always been passionately concerned with the welfare of the show border collie and my aim is to breed typical, healthy specimens of the breed. Despite having twenty five years experience in the show world, I was anxious to get as much clarification as possible about the border collie Breed Standard, as laid down by the Kennel Club. My partner Felix Cosme and I needed a guideline because we wanted to breed our own strain, otherwise we would be working in the dark.

With this in mind, we decided to serve on the Border Collie Club of Great Britain, hoping we could contribute our experience, as well as receive the help we needed. Full discussion of the standard was anticipated at the 1978 annual general meeting, but we were to be disappointed. The subject was very lightly touched upon and little interest seemed to be shown in tightening up requirements, or making it more accessible to the novice. In fact, the chairman told us that they would not be tightening up the standard because a border collie might be bred that was not covered by the standard and then the Kennel Club would have to make alterations.

The unfinished amended standard that was circulated at that time was much criticised. All round judges complained that in the ring there was such a variety of types and the standard gave very little guidance for those meeting the breed for the first time. Consequently, most of the judges at open shows left the borders out of the winning finals because the dogs they saw had not been described in the standard.

The 1986 Breed Standard leaves a great deal to the imagination and the whim of the breeder. I personally feel it should be even more comprehensive allowing no loopholes and with nothing left to chance so that untypical types cannot be accepted in the breed. There is a sincere wish among enthusiasts that the border collie should not be altered in any way so that the breed retains the characteristics we know and love. A standard should have been composed that covered every angle, with no chance for deviation at all. There have been many who have said: "It is too early to tie down a standard". It is never too early for the knowledgeable to guide the novices.

Physiology of the
border collie

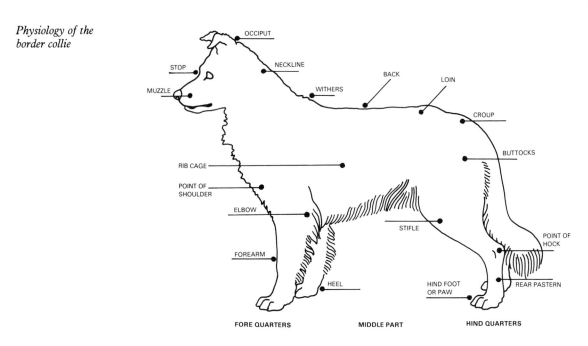

Left to their own devices, the unscrupulous breeders and the idiosyncrasies of fashion would have altered the breed out of all recognition. But the border collie has been in existence for so many years, it should not be too complicated to aim for a recognised middle type.

The Border Collie Breed Standard

GENERAL APPEARANCE: Well proportioned, smooth outline showing quality, gracefulness and perfect balance, combined with sufficient substance to give impression of endurance. Any tendency to coarseness or weediness, undesirable.

CHARACTERISTICS: Tenacious, hardworking sheepdog of great tractability.

TEMPERAMENT: Keen, alert, responsive and intelligent. Neither nervous nor aggressive.

HEAD & SKULL: Skull fairly broad, occiput not pronounced. Cheeks not full or rounded. Muzzle, tapering to nose, moderately short and strong. Skull and foreface approximately equal in length. Stop very distinct. Nose

Ideal length of muzzle.
Flat skull, balanced head

No Stop.

Too short in the muzzle.
Domed skull.

Too long in the muzzle.

black, except in brown or chocolate colour when it may be brown. In blues nose should be slate colour. Nostrils well developed.

★ There is an error in the official Breed Standard and it states: cheeks full or rounded. I have corrected this here, and warn all show people to make a note of this misleading mistake.

EYES: Set wide apart, oval shaped, of moderate size, brown in colour except in merles where one or both or part of one or both may be blue. Expression mild, keen, alert and intelligent.

EARS: Medium size and texture, set well apart. Carried erect or semi-erect and sensitive in use.

MOUTH: Teeth and jaws strong with a perfect, regular and complete scissor bite, i.e. upper teeth closely overlapping lower teeth and set square to the jaws.

NECK: Of good length, strong and muscular, slightly arched and broadening to shoulders.

FOREQUARTERS: Front legs parallel when viewed from front, pasterns slightly sloping when viewed from side. Bone strong but not heavy. Shoulders well laid back, elbows close to body.

BODY: Athletic in appearance, ribs well sprung, chest deep and rather broad, loins deep and muscular, but not tucked up. Body slightly longer than height at shoulder.

HINDQUARTERS: Broad, muscular, in profile sloping gracefully to set on of tail. Thighs long, deep and muscular with well turned stifles and strong well let down hocks. From hock to ground, hindlegs well boned and parallel when viewed from rear.

FEET: Oval in shape, pads deep, strong and sound, toes arched and close together. Nails short and strong.

TAIL: Moderately long, the bone reaching at least to hock, set on low, well furnished and with an upward swirl towards the end, completing graceful contour and balance of dog. Tail may be raised in excitement, never carried over back.

GAIT/MOVEMENT: Free, smooth and tireless, with minimum lift of feet, conveying impression of ability to move with great stealth and speed.

COAT: Two varieties: 1) Moderately long. 2) Smooth. In both, topcoat dense and medium textured, undercoat soft and dense giving good weather resistance. In moderately long coated variety, abundant coat forms mane, breeching and brush. On face, ears, forelegs (except for feather), hindlegs from hock to ground, hair should be short and smooth.

COLOUR: Variety of colours permissible. White should never predominate.

SIZE: Ideal height: Dogs 53 cms (21 ins); Bitches slightly less.

FAULTS: Any departure from the foregoing points should be considered a fault and the seriousness with which the fault should be regarded should be in exact proportion to its degree.

NOTE: Male animals should have two apparently normal testicles fully descended into the scrotum.

This present standard does give a guideline to the specialist judges, but I do feel that judges new to the breed, need one or two points clarifying. There is such a wide variety of colours, pigmentation and eye colour that is acceptable, that the combinations should be specified in much more detail. Colouring should be of secondary importance when deciding on a breeding programme and the judges who might penalise a colour combination that they are not familiar with, should be made aware of the wide range allowed. In so many other breeds there are colours that are not desired or even allowed, so the colour combinations that we can breed should be mentioned in detail rather than the stark: 'Variety of colour permissible. White should never predominate.' The situation could arise that only black and white border collies with dark brown eyes are placed in the winning line-up. So many people visualise the border collie as a black and white animal with white blaze, collar, chest and four white feet. They must be informed and educated to accept the rest of the range. It is not sufficient information to put in a standard: 'a variety of colours are permissible' especially for all round judges who judge the working group at championship shows. When confronted by a best of breed winner that is either tri-colour, blue merle, red merle or red and white, they could well be overlooked because the judge was not aware of the colour combination.

The present standard asks for all colours other than merles to have brown eye colour. But there are many shades of brown from the very dark to the nearly yellow. Yet many judges mention in their critiques that the eye colour was too light. So long as the eyes can be described as brown – light brown, medium brown, or dark brown – it cannot be incorrect.

I would also like to see mention of dappling on the white parts of the legs and muzzle in the black and white and the red and white. I have been asked

These markings are very
popular with the white
blaze, white muzzle, white
collar, white chest and white
feet and tail tip. This applies
equally with a black or red coat.

Mismarkings where the head
is white and there are patchy
white markings over the body.
The Breed Standard states that
white colouring should not
predominate.

The merle patterning can
be seen in the red merle and the
blue merle. The merle dogs
sometimes have split eye colour.

Ticking or dappling is very attractive and a dog or bitch with these markings should not be penalised.

A black border collie with very little white markings can be just as attractive as the one with white markings, so long as the construction is good.

Black/light shading for red and whites. The tri-colour is next in popularity in the show ring, red rather than a grey third colour, makes the dog more attractive.

many times if that is allowed as there is no mention of dappling in the standard. In the Gait/Movement section it mentions the 'ability to move with great stealth and speed' This should convey the impression that the working, crouching movement is typical of the breed. But in no way should it be associated with cringing or cowering, because of poor temperament.

When I judged border collies in Germany, several imports were brought into the ring to be judged. Many were so untypical that it was difficult to tell if they were true border collies. Their movement was upright and stilted. Then a handsome border collie came into the open class. He had been brought from a farm in Germany quite recently and he looked very impressive. He stood with his head level with his back, with an alert expression, searching with a piercing eye for any sheep that might be about. His ears were so active, tipped but moving to catch every sound. He moved as if he was working, stifles well bent, and forequarters nearly bent double. I made him my best of breed winner. Later when talking to his owner, a farmer who regularly worked his dogs, I told him how much I admired his beautiful border collie. He told me that no German judge would accept the movement, they would call it cringing, and as he was continually using his ears, he would also be penalised for that. In Germany the border collie ears must be held still like the rough collie's ears. I am pleased our standard requires ears to be 'carried erect or semi-erect and sensitive in use.' I was also told that the Germans would not accept erect ears so I sent the farmer a copy of our standard. He carried it with him to shows, even to a show in Switzerland, but it made no difference.

The standard for the neck states it must be of good length, strong and muscular, slightly arched and broadening to shoulders. A balanced border should have a strong and supple neck, not too short and certainly not too long. Markings sometimes give the illusion that the neck is longer than it is, especially if the white collar markings come well over the shoulders. Similarly, a border with no white collar can give the impression of being stuffy in neck. A good depth of brisket is important, with well sprung ribcage. Such an active dog needs plenty of heart and lung room. There are too many shelly finely made borders being bred and shown. Maturity will sometimes help development, but no finely built weedy borders should be mated to similar partners. Also, a finely built bitch can benefit from having a litter so long as she is mated to a well made, good boned dog, the puppies could be an improvement on the dam.

The question then arises of where to go to produce these show winning borders that comply with the standard, for the standard is our guide. Many breeders go back to the working stock but they do not always have the success they are looking for. Problems that did not show in the dog of their

The border collie Breed Standard states that ears can be carried errect or semi-errect So all three of these variations are acceptable

A. Ears carried errect

B. Tip-ears

C. Drop ears

This is a good specimen of the border collie as described in the Breed Standard. It is balanced when standing four square and has a good level back sloping from the withers with no drop away. It has a good bend of stifle and tail set. The head is nicely balanced with good stop and the muzzle is the correct depth.

This dog is too short in the back, making it look very unbalanced. As a junior it would have looked very leggy. On the move it would short step badly. The head is too heavy for the body, with no stop and a deep muzzle giving the look of a coarse head.

This dog has a completely wrong shaped head – too deep in the muzzle and no stop. It is long in body and noticeably dipping behind the withers. It is over developed at the rear and the mismarking makes the dog look longer than it is.

This dog is too long in the loin. Sloping stop making a very fine muzzle. With the length of back and no depth of brisket, the dog could be called shelly.

Black and white bitch showing very poor rear construction.
There is no depth of brisket and the bone is not good. She has nice dark eyes and a good flat skull

choice could well have been present in the stud dog's litter brothers and sisters. With more information about the ancestors of the present day dogs and bitches, we should be much more aware of what could be produced from different combinations. Good looking stud dogs only one or two generations away from working stock can have brothers and sisters that in no way comply with the standard. That is why judges are now confronted with such a wide variety of types.

We also need more guidance on border collie topline and tail set. We are informed that hindquarters must be broad, muscular, in profile sloping gracefully to set on of tail. But it would certainly help to mention that topline level should have no drop behind the withers and should slope gracefully to set on of tail. Poor toplines can be seen quite often in the ring, showing weakness. A border collie too long in body with a sway back – dipping of topline between the withers and hip bone – used at stud can soon produce this weakness in his or her offspring as has occured in other breeds.

CHAPTER FOUR

Buying a Show Puppy

THERE are still a few breeders who plan to produce their litters entirely for the show ring, though most breeders hope that the puppies they sell will be either used for obedience, trials, or working, with a percentage going into the show world. Therefore it is their policy to register litters with the International Sheep Dog Society and the Kennel Club. At Beagold we only have three dogs registered with the ISDS and KC, the others are just KC registered for the show ring.

When choosing a border collie puppy for show, it is wise to pay great attention to temperament and type. The pup must also be healthy, sturdy and well reared with clean bright eyes and sweet smelling clean ears. The puppy should be plump and the bones of the legs straight. It should have a cheerful inquisitive and interested character. The mouth should have a scissor bite and the baby teeth must be clean. The coat should be shiny and free from dandruff or parasites.

The next thing to assess is show potential. At the age of eight weeks when most puppies are purchased it is terribly important for the puppy to have a level topline with a low set tail, the tail should have no bone knots or kinks. Gently encourage the puppy to pick a titbit off the floor, its neck should be flexible and when reaching for the titbit it should not need to bend its front legs. Front legs should be parallel even at this early age and rear bend of stifle should be noticeable. The hocks must also be parallel when viewed from behind. Feathering should just begin to show on tail, rear, and slightly longer around the ruff. I like to pick the puppy with the smallest ears, already being held in a lifted position when attracted by sudden noise. The shape of head is important. It should have a noticeable stop and the skull should be flat. The eyes should be dark and bright in the black and white borders and noticeably brown in the red and white. The eyes should not be too light in the tri-colour, especially when the tri is white, brown and black.

We prefer to sell a show puppy at four months of age, then more signs of quality have developed. The border collie alters so much from eight weeks to maturity. When we breed from our own stock either in-breeding or line-breeding, we know what to expect. Each litter has similar characteristics of type. In fact, from several litters we expect to see one with a white edge to its ear, we also expect tri-colour and black and white. Ear carriage also varies, some excellent, others not so good.

There are breeders who now go in for the unusual colours, the blue merles, the red merles, red and white, some that even have sable in the mixture of colour in their coat. It is yet to be seen whether judges at championship shows will accept these other colours. Black and white are still most commonly picked for best of breed, so it is still a gamble when chosing a show puppy. Judges are mostly in favour of dark brown eyes too, they take into account the majority of other breeds in the show ring where dark eyes are a necessity.

I have not yet mentioned the smooth coated border collie. There is a marked difference in this type, they have no feathering, their coat is smooth and short and they have no full ruff. When the border collie is out of coat, and they certainly do drop everything at their first moulting which usually happens when they are just over a year, they can be taken for a smooth collie. In fact, one judge gave the trophy for best smooth border collie at a club show to a long coated dog that was out of coat. That is how easy it is to make the mistake.

Here again, I do not think the more unusual smooth coated border collie is likely to have so much success in the show ring as its longer-coated counterpart. Yet in most other respects, the smooth coated border is like the longer coated in shape and conformation. Whatever type has gone into the make-up of the smooth seen around the show ring at the present time, is certainly foreign to the long coated types. Many look like cross breds. The black and white borders seem to have settled into a similar mould with slight differences in make-up, shape and movement, but unmistakable types have been bred. It is the coloured borders that sometimes look like another breed. All over long blue merle coats give the impression of coming from rough collies or shelties. Texture of coat is also suspect. The red merle, and red and white sometimes do not have the appearance of the correct border collie, only one or two that reach the show ring are similar in all other respects to their black and white and tri-coloured brothers and sisters.

Basic training for the show ring must start very early for the puppy and in a later chapter I will go into this in more detail. Four or five times a day the puppy should be gently encouraged to stand for inspection. Just a few minutes training each time, but the same words must be used. No force must be used on the young pup. All you need to do is gently stroke the puppy's tail down so that it gets into the habit of holding its tail at the correct angle right from the beginning. We start training our puppies for show at four weeks of age and so long as the new owner continues with the same instructions and training when the puppy is bought at eight weeks, there is no reason why it should have any problems when it finally reaches the show ring.

We rarely buy puppies in, only on the odd occasion when we need new blood, or have a puppy returned in lieu of a stud fee. But we always let the newcomer get accustomed to our way of life and its new environment before we start training. As soon as we feel that the puppy has acclimatised to its new life and feels secure, we start the training. We also ask for a menu, so that we can continue to feed the puppy the same diet that it has been used to. A change of diet at this stage could easily upset its digestive system. After a few weeks we gradually change to the food that we give to our dogs. As we have breeding kennels we isolate the puppy for three weeks to make sure that it is completely free from infection before it associates with our dogs.

We restrict the exercise given to young puppies and advise new owners to do the same. Their food intake is needed to build up sound limbs, good muscle, and a well covered body, and should not be wasted away by too much exercise. A puppy that is allowed to chase about all day with no restrictions will grow like a weed, leggy and thin. If it develops an upset tummy or goes off its food during this fast growing period, it will have nothing to fall back on and end up a poor doer. We allow the pups as much exercise as they want for a couple of hours in complete freedom, then they are encouraged to sleep. Two hours later they are ready and keen to start playing again. This play time lasts until they have their evening meal and then they are quite happy to settle for the night. As the pups grow older the play time is extended, until they are adults. Then from early morning to evening they are out in the compounds and being exercised in the fields.

During this period the training continues, for free exercise on grass and walking on roads on the lead is all preparation for the show ring. So when the puppy is over six months and enters its first show, nothing appears frightening. It has encountered all the different sights and sounds and accepts them without bother. We groom on the table so that the pup associates jumping on the table with jumping up on to a bench. Car journeys, meeting people and being in close contact with other dogs are all part of the young pup's education, so when it enters the show ring it performs like a seasoned campaigner.

CHAPTER FIVE

Show Preparation

THE border collie is a very easy breed to keep in spotless condition. Some might imagine that with the length and texture of coat, with feathering confined to the legs, a bushy tail and ruff, that there is no need to put a brush and comb near the dog. They are wrong. All dogs enjoy and benefit from a thorough grooming session. They squirm and wriggle as the brush goes the length of their back and after a few minutes of long strokes, the coat gleams.

I comb the feathering, which if left, will tangle badly. It is also necessary to regularly comb and brush behind the ears, the bushy tail and the feathering on the legs. The finished product looks good in the show ring, and I am pleased to say that there are now many owners that put time and effort into the presentation of the dogs.

Our border collies keep themselves very clean, even after a long walk in wet weather the mud and dirt soon falls off them and all that is needed is a brush all over and they look as good as new. When we are taking a dog to a show a little bit of extra care needs to be put into the coat to make it look its best. Should there be any question of dirt left in the coat, or the white markings looking a little dingy, we give the dog a bath. But we do not consider that all over bathing does the coat a lot of good. In fact, if the dog is bathed too frequently the coat gets dry as all the natural oils are washed away. If an all over bath is not necessary, we just wash the white parts with a canine shampoo, usually Vetzyme shampoo. This is rubbed in with a sponge, rinsed and then dried which soon has the white coat looking bright and clean.

The ears need very little attention. They must be clean and sweet smelling, with no hair growing down into the ear passage.

It all depends on the dogs' diet, whether the teeth will need to be cleaned. If tartar does collect, I use a tooth scraper and brush them with Eucryl Powder to clean off any debris around the gums. By keeping the dog's teeth free of tartar, we avoid problems of decay, right up to old age. The border collie is a notorious chewer: wood, wire, steel feeding bowls and tree bark are all in their diet. Our dogs have silver markings on their teeth from chewing their steel feeding bowls and the wire fence and it is not at all unusual to see fairly young border collies with broken teeth. This is not because they are confined in small enclosures, when they are out in the fields they pick up anything removable and chew to their heart's content.

The feet should be examined regularly as mud can clog the paws and cause sores. I use scissors to keep the feet clear of hair and so it only takes a minute to wash and dry them. I just trim the hair so that the paws are nicely rounded.

The nails are usually worn down with the normal active movement of the border but if the dog is only exercised on soft ground, then it is necessary to cut nails fairly short so that the foot does not look splayed. Be careful that you do not cut the quick, it is only the white tip that needs cutting. If it bleeds, a quick dab of iodine will stop the flow.

I also trim the hair from toe to hock, in a similar way to the presentation of the rough collie and shetland sheepdog. As the dog moves down the show ring a tidy pair of hocks looks much nicer and neater than if they are left untidy and straggly.

An all over thorough grooming with a hard brush should leave the hair like silk. The ruff and fringes might need the comb through them, in case they have tangles or a mat of dead hair. Tease out the matt with the comb, then comb through properly. The great advantage of the border collie is that it needs very little cosmetic alterations to its natural coat. The border collie has a complete moult when it is about fourteen months of age. Great tufts of hair come out and it is important to groom all this dead hair out. Regular brushing will encourage the new hair to grow. We also find that once a year they lose a lot of hair, but once it is combed away there is only the new growing hair left. As the border grows older they moult once a year but never seem to lose as much of their coat as that first moult. If they are kept healthy and groomed regularly they do not lose coat, other than once a year, which is easy to cope with.

CHAPTER SIX

Show Presentation

AS a new breed in the beauty show ring, no one particular person should need to dictate what method of presentation should be applied when showing your border collie. Some owners prefer to use the method similar to posing the German Shepherd, others bring their dogs into the show ring and attempt to pose them like shetland sheepdogs, or rough and smooth coated collies. I personally consider that which ever way you choose, the end result should be the same. The dog should be presented to the judge in such a manner as to convey the standard as a beautiful picture, with no need to describe it in words.

If you wish to stack your border you should be at liberty to do so. The idea is to emphasise the dog's good points and camouflage his faults but without interfering with the other exhibits in the ring. If the method you use upsets another dog and exhibitor, then it is the wrong method. When toys are thrown about or squeaky objects used to keep the dog amused and alert, it can often affect the other dogs and put them off the job in hand. The border collie is naturally an alert and attentive dog, its eyes follow its owner's every move, without the need for added enticements such as liver and other titbits to hold its attention. In fact, you can end up doing yourself no favours. The judge might be looking at the dog's front to see if it has the correct depth of brisket and whether its front legs are parallel and it is most annoying if the dog suddenly lunges forward to be fed. These intelligent dogs hear a command in the obedience ring and they rush to do their owner's bidding. Surely asking them to stand for a minute's inspection by the judge, is not beyond their capabilities.

When standing the dog you can see if it is standing ten to two, or east-west, some dogs stand like that although they have good straight fronts. A dog drawn into the stand can also look cow-hocked, just a little extra attention or a move to re-stand it can make all the difference when the judge is looking for her winners. When moving your dog around the ring, do make sure you are not crowding the dog in front. If you are a slow mover, or your dog is, glance behind to see if you are stopping the person behind you from moving

*Dogs presented ready for
the judge's final assessment.*

*The different methods
of presentation
are highlighted here.
The first handler
is using titbits, the
second has the collar
up behind the dog's ears
and is holding his head
up. The third has the
dog standing on a loose
lead but is encouraging
stance with a titbit
in her pocket. The fourth
is holding the dog on a
loose lead and talking to
it to hold its attention.*

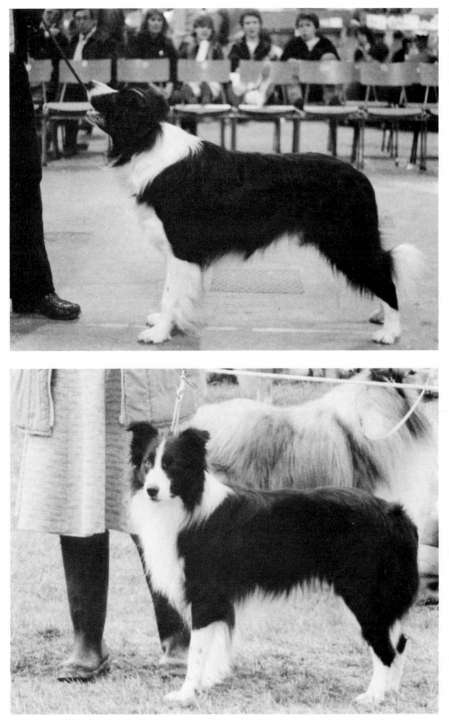

Show Champion Huntroyde Beau Brummel at Sanrian, standing well on a loose lead with his attention fixed on his handler

Alpha of Beesting showing to perfection. The handler has obviously studied the dog well and knows that he stands without over-handling and placing of his legs. A slightly taut lead reminds him that he must stay in position. His snow white coat shows up his black coat to perfection.

fast. When I am judging I do not think the mad dash around the ring about five or six times shows anything important, only the fact that the owner can move fast. It is much more sensible to take your dog at a steady pace. Moving the dog up the ring to see rear action at any pace and bringing it back towards the judge shows much more information about the dog's conformation on the move than the side movement, although both are needed to properly assess the worth of each exhibit.

If I notice the person behind me wishes to pace their dog faster than mine will go, I stand back and let the person go ahead. It shows good sportsmanship and not all judges wish to see the dog dashing around the ring at breakneck speed, they might well appreciate your steady slower movement and place you higher than the tearaway. It is only when the steward hands you your prize card that you can afford to relax. Up until then, the judge can change his mind at any second, especially when there is very little between the dogs. A dog that is handled well, presented in immaculate condition and behaves and cooperates with judge and handler can sometimes sway the decision in its favour, so all the hours of training spent to build up a working rapport with your dog pays off in the end.

CHAPTER SEVEN

The Show Ring

THERE was a time several years ago, when a novice exhibitor would not have dreamt of taking an untrained, ungroomed dog into the show ring and then expect to win. The thought of taking the dog to compete at anything as grand as a championship show would not have entered their mind. Most new owners would try their puppy or young adult at the local exemption show. This is where they would meet with other novice owners all equally nervous, unsure of themselves, and of their dog's behaviour in the show ring.

Exemption means that the show organisers have obtained a licence from the Kennel Club to hold the dog show in aid of a good cause, usually for a Rescue Scheme or Guide Dogs for the Blind, and it is exempt from Kennel Club rules. Four pedigree classes are classified with as many novelty classes as they wish to put on. The atmosphere is friendly and relaxed and the classes are usually large with a variety of breeds being shown. The very nervous novice would probably take a sidelong glance at the other exhibits and sadly admit that they had no chance of winning and their adored pet did not look quite so outstanding as they had first imagined. Imagine their delight if the judge decides their pet is worthy of a prize card, even if it had not been previously show-trained. This first win can easily spur a dog owner to try again, perhaps at a sanction show which has classes for pedigree dogs with no novelty classes and is run by a dog society. Their first prize card will be a treasured memento.

A little higher up the hierarchy of dog shows is the members limited show. These are friendly well run shows where everyone knows everyone else. The members who have more experience of showing, are always willing to give newcomers a helping hand. Members have donated trophies and cups to be won at every show which makes it very rewarding for the newcomer who has the chance to win their first challenge trophy.

By this time, they will have caught the show going bug and will want to try for higher stakes, leading up to the open show. This class of show is open to all and in the breed classes fellow competitors will be regular show going exhibitors. Many societies now classify border collie classes, and receive excellent entries. This could well be the first opportunity to compete in classes with other border collies under a specialist or all round judge. At open shows there are usually four or five classes for each breed, usually divided into puppy, novice, graduate, or open for dog and bitch. A first prize card win in one or two open show classes will give confirmation to the novice that they have a good specimen of the breed and the temptation is then to enter a championship show. A first prize win in minor puppy, puppy, junior, post graduate, limit and open class at this level qualifies for entry at Crufts, the world's most famous dog show. Here, you will find a completely different world. The competition is intense and there is exciting talk of challenge certificates, group wins, top stud dogs, brood bitches that regularly produce champion offspring, good judges and bad judges – a language that will only become familiar after years of competing at the top level.

There are so many frightening things that can happen at championship shows, like the enormous marquees flapping noisily in the high winds and even crashing to the ground. The dog showing crowd encounter storms, rain, mud, brilliant sunshine and burning heat. There are loudspeaker announce-ments throughout the day and it always surprises me how many requests there are in the summer to rescue dogs from cars that have become like ovens. Too many thoughtless owners forget their unfortunate dogs and spend time in the bar, while their prize exhibits suffer in the car. All these harrassments and bewildering experiences have to be encountered and it is no wonder that a young puppy has a job to cope. Even a seasoned show dog finds the hustle and bustle quite unnerving, especially if a belated arrival means a quick dash into the show ring pulled along by an irate owner.

The first thing I would suggest is to allow plenty of time. Collect all the necessary equipment, like drinking bowl, water, towel, brush and comb. We used to use chalk to whiten up the white parts of a dog's coat, but there is now a Kennel Club rule banning it. If you need to feed a young dog during the show day, remember a dish of food. Some people use a special show lead, others don't bother and use the everyday lead and collar. If the puppy tends to be car sick there are some good tablets that can be given an hour before the journey. These can be bought at dog shows and are very effective. Shaws Travel Sickness tablets come in two strengths, for puppies and for adults.

If it is a championship show you must bench your dog. That means fasten the dog's lead to the bench and give him a drink of water. Then make sure you know where the ring is, so that when the time comes for you to take your place, you are not searching the huge venue, sometimes even missing a class. The catalogue will give you all the information you need and sometimes has a map of the area locating toilets, exercise places and refreshment tents. This is when the show is outside; there will also be information about wet weather

Entries at Windsor championship show.

accommodation. Some judges retreat immediately to their allocated wet weather tent, at the first signs of rain, others don wellies, rain hat and coat and stick it out, with the soaked exhibitors shivering and trying to do their best with unhappy wet dogs.

The West of England Ladies championship show is the first outside show to be held in April, and it usually heralds a snow storm or high winds and bitter cold. But there have been times when luck has been with us, and the beautiful venue at the Three Counties Showground at Malvern, Worcestershire has been bathed in sunshine. It is a popular venue and several championship shows are held there. The winter venues present no problems for the border collies, the breed seems to adjust easily to inside and outside shows. With their temperament and character, even the noise and bustle of Earls Court, the home of Crufts, presents no particular problems. None of the dogs first shown there were affected by the noise and they accepted the benches and crowds as if they had encountered such congestion all their lives. But many of the dogs that were entered at this most important and prestigious show, should have had some basic ring training. Dogs were allowed to crowd each other when moving around the ring, some even sniffed and annoyed the dogs in front which put them off showing correctly.

When you arrive for the first time in the ring, the steward will give you your number and you will be told where to stand with your dog. Space yourself, giving the person and the dog in front of you plenty of room, the same as you would expect from the person behind you. The judge might ask you all to move around the ring together. This is a test especially for the border collie as it is a natural instinct to chase anything that is in front. So you must ensure that you are firmly in control. Trouble will result if the dog in front happens to resent another coming up too close behind, so it is wise to keep your distance.

The judge will then call each exhibitor and their dog into the centre of the ring, and ask you to stand your dog for inspection. Here again, your dog should be trained to stand for a few minutes while the judge goes over him. There should be no need to bait the dog with titbits, squeaky toys, or rustle paper. This is very offputting for the judge, and could well annoy other dogs. The judge will make allowances for a puppy that tries to jump up and greet him, but then the pup will be expected to stand still. A good handler can make a dog look better than it is, but a bad handler will make a dog look worse than it is.

Presentation is also important. Even though the border collie is a working breed, the judge will not expect the dog to be tangled and dirty. When it is

Joyce Collis and partner Felix Cosme. Felix always acts as Steward when Joyce is judging.

JUDGES & STEWARDS

working in the fields or out for a run, it can get as dirty as it likes. But when you are presenting your dog in the beauty ring, it should smell sweet and look gleamingly clean. No one should expect to win with a dog that has not been groomed or bathed and yet there are many that have such expectations. When they are disappointed they usually accuse the judge of being biased. Do not make excuses if your dog does not win. Take another look at him and ask yourself honestly if you really deserved to win. Did your dog move correctly, did he behave? Your dog might only have a couple of minor faults, but assessed with bad showmanship, this could well have swayed the judge's decision. The other dogs in the competition might have had minor faults which were outweighed by being beautifully presented, well handled and moving correctly. By showing good sportsmanship and trying again, the decision might be reversed next time, especially if your dog is better trained.

Some exhibitors are never honest with themselves, they blame the poor venue, the noise in the hall and the incompetence of the judge. The judge comes in for all sorts of complaints, either he is a friend of the winner, or his dog sired the winner's dog. Another reason given is that the judge has used the winning dog at stud. If the judge is honest and puts up a dog that he considers worthy of the title of champion, then that is the type the judge likes and no doubt it would be the dog picked to mate his bitch. The progeny of the stud dog might also be winners and if placed, the judge is to be congratulated on having a good eye for type. The protesters might be acting stupidly, but there is no reason for the judge to do the same, or use a lesser dog at stud because of what people might say.

There are many pitfalls leading up the ladder of success, but hard work, dedication and above all, luck, will keep you trying again and again for those green cards that will give your dog the title show champion. It is usually from the open class at championship shows that the top winners are chosen and by the time you are ready to compete in these top classes, your dog or bitch is usually mature, trained and well deserves the honour. Sometimes an early flyer will beat the older dogs by being ring-trained, mature and well presented. If you win in your class you will be called back to compete against all the other unbeaten dogs. From this line-up the challenge certificate and reserve challenge certificate winners are chosen. The bitches are then judged, and the challenge certificate winning bitch is called in to compete for best of breed. By winning this you are then expected to compete in the working group ring with the other best of breed winners. At the present time, only two border collies have won reserve in the working group, our Show Champion Tilehouse Cassius of Beagold was the first and then in 1984 Show Champion Melodor Flurry won reserve in the working group at Crufts.

Members of the International Sheep Dog Society, the Kennel Club and three committee members of the Border Collie Club of Great Britain, and the Southern Border Collie Club decided that the border collie should only receive the title show champion when it won at Kennel Club championship shows and should only receive the full champion title after it had completed a test to prove that it could also work. The border collie is the only breed in the working group that has to qualify its capabilities for work before being allowed the full title. Only one dog so far has proved its capabilities for work in the field, but has not gained any titles in the show ring, and that is Dr. Leigh's Fordrought Fen.

The working test is not difficult for those dogs who have daily contact with sheep. Fen was one of the few show dogs who had a will to work. But there are so many others who have never seen sheep, and most of us realise that what they have never known, they will not miss. A typical example of the difference in temperament of some of the borders today is the two I was watching at an open show. Mary Gascoigne's Gambit of Kathmick, sired by Mac out of Twig and obviously from strong working stock, would have been more at home in the fields. He showed no interest whatsoever in showing off his good points to the judge and he paid no attention at all to his owner's commands. His whole attention and interest was fixed on the sparrows flying around the hall, searching for crumbs and titbits. Never once did his attention waver from the birds, he watched them up above and on the ground. It was a fascinating sight, but most frustrating for the owner. When the judge wasn't, looking his stance was perfect. He looked alert, quivering with excitement – a real picture. The best of breed winner was a beautifully made bitch puppy, Mrs Whittington's Turn Again Tod. One would have thought she was from generations of show dogs, her construction and presentation was excellent. She behaved superbly, moved well, and stood for inspection like a statue. Although her sire was a show dog, Whenway Rhys of Mizanne, he was only slightly removed from working stock and her dam was Dellaridges Dreamboat, who was not at all well known in the show ring. That was how it was.

Today the exhibitor arrives at a championship show and quite unconcernedly remarks that this is their puppy's first every show, and of course, they have never been to one either. Their border collie has no training whatsoever and is often unruly. In some cases the judge has to struggle with the lively puppy as he tries to check its mouth and its construction. In some cases, the young dog is brought into the championship show ring straight from obedience classes or working sheep. No wonder some judges who have not encountered the breed too often before are puzzled as to the qualifications and judging standard of this breed. But there are many judges who understand the situation and judge accordingly. They recognise the fact that the untrained puppy is of excellent type, regardless of the unusual movement, they appreciate that if the puppy is obedience trained it will move close to its owner's sides, looking up continually for instruction and they understand that creeping, crouching movement of some border collies means that the dog would rather be out in the fields working.

In some instances some of the excellent border collies are penalised because they do not conform to the recognised behaviour of the show dogs in the working group at shows. With such intelligent animals, it is a shame they have not been given a few hours of instruction before they are bought into the show ring. After all, no dog would be taken into an obedience championship show without specialised training for the job it was asked to perform.

We take our young border pups to a very well run training school. The basic collar and lead training has already taken place in our own garden. But the border pup needs to be among other dogs, and he must learn to ignore them while he is in the show ring. A common tendency is for the border pup to dart out at another dog as it walks by. This has to be corrected immediately before it becomes a habit. A quick choke on the chain and a command of either 'No' or 'Leave', every time this happens, will soon correct the natural inclination to catch anything that passes by.

As time goes by more and more borders adjust to the show ring, so it is obvious that border collie owners enjoy showing and are spending more time teaching their dogs and bitches ring manners.

*The author
Joyce Collis conducting
events at Windsor
Championship show.*

CHAPTER EIGHT

Judging

I FIND judging a most rewarding experience. In fact, I prefer my judging appointments even more than exhibiting my own dogs. My first appointment to judge border collies was in 1980 at the Border Collie Club of Great Britain show at the Weedon Village Hall, Northants.

A large spacious hall, seemed even larger because of the few dogs and bitches that had entered the show ring. In fact the eighty seven dogs made a total of one hundred and forty four entries, with many of them coming from the obedience classes. With only four years of recognition behind the breeders of show border collies, most of the other dogs were trained for obedience only and moved as they would in the obedience class, close to heel and gazing up into the face of their handler for further instruction. I made allowances for that, as it was not too difficult to catch glimpses of sound movement when they crouched and glided up and down the hall. Judging border collies was a challenge at that time and one I was keen to accept. There were still so many exhibitors who thought showing border collies was a waste of time. But they still wanted to try out the new discipline, regardless. Unfortunately very few had even studied the standard, or wished to. They queried how a border collie could be judged on beauty alone and how could a judge not place a good moving, well coated, strongly built dog or bitch? What more was there to assess?

Critiques that contained such statements as: poor front (when the dog stands noticeably at ten to two) incorrect shaped head, high set tail, cow hocks, overshot or undershot bite, would not stop a dog from doing the job it was born to do, it was a working dog. There were many with these faults, some heads resembled that of the rough collie, there were also dobermann shaped heads and even the stronger square head resembling that of the labrador. No one had bred dogs solely for show, and it certainly was noticeable in those early days.

In 1982 the border collie was given challenge certificates for the first time at Crufts. As I have mentioned earlier, Harry Glover, the president of the Border Club of Great Britain was to be given the honour of judging and

Bill Finlay presents Felix Cosme with the border collie headed crook for winning the challenge certificate and best of breed at the National Working Breeds championship show, making Tilehouse Cassius at Beagold the first ever show champion.

giving out challenge certificates for the first time. The Crufts catalogue was printed with his name as the officiating judge but Mrs Catherine Sutton had to be offered the appointment in his place. The entry was excellent with fifty seven dogs and bitches making seventy eight entries. We were very proud to win the first dog challenge certificate and best of breed with Tilehouse Cassius at Beagold and Felix Cosme handling. The bitch ticket was one by Eric Broadhurst's Tracelyn Gal, handled by the owner.

Mrs Catherine Sutton certainly received an unusual entry, one that must have been a definite first in her wide experience as an international championship show judge. There were all shapes and sizes with some borders not many months away from working sheep in the fields as well as a number of obedience workers. We were one of the few kennels with dogs trained solely for the show ring. Cassius was expertly handled and behaved like a show dog. He stood out so noticeably, his coat groomed to perfection and he was completely at home.

In 1983 I was honoured to be the first specialist judge to give challenge certificates at Crufts. As Cassius had gained his title and was the winner of 1982 Crufts Show, we were asked to supply a photograph of him to go in the catalogue. We chose a photograph of him with his handler Felix and Bill

Show Champion
Tork of Whenway.

Show Champion
Kathmik Griff.

Finlay, the judge who had given Cassius his title. Mr Finlay had presented Felix with a crook he had made himself, with the head of a border collie carved for the handle. This is now a treasured possession. The entry for Crufts 1983 was no larger than the previous year. As with the few sets of challenge certificates on offer throughout the previous year, only those winners of the first prize in puppy, junior, post graduate, limit and the open class would have qualified to enter at Crufts. The number was further reduced because many of the first prize winners had won several times throughout the year. There were forty five dogs and bitches from fifty one entries.

I had my work cut out to find typical, good quality specimens of the breed. There were only one or two that had been trained for the show ring, so the strange noises and unfamiliar environment made judging difficult. I found my best of breed winner in Tork of Whenway, owned by Sheena and Bruce Kilsby and handled by Bruce. Tork is now a show champion. He was a well made strong dog, with a well balanced good type head and a nice alert expression. He had a good deep brisket level topline and the right length of loin. He did not have the glamorous white markings, but that did not detract from his overall quality. His movement was not his fortune, he weaved and raced around the ring, only giving me slight glimpses of what could be considered sound movement. Later when he calmed down slightly, he added more challenge certificates to his credit.

The open dog class had several who would have given a better performance out in the fields and with very little choice, I settled for Tork's runaway circle of the ring. He gained enough good points on his sound construction to beat the reserve challenge certificate winner, Kathmick Griff. Mary Gascoigne's dog was another soundly constructed type with a lively character. He has also gained his show champion title since. Griff was a handsome tri-colour dog, very hard to handle and difficult to assess. He also circled the ring as if he was out in the fields working sheep.

My best bitch was Mr and Mrs Lewin's Mizanne the Witch who is now a show champion. She is a beautifully made prick-eared bitch, with an excellent feminine head, good alert expression, lovely outline and movement that is more restrained than the dogs. She won well, but when it came to the final decision, several judges were unable to accept the pricked ears, although they are accepted in the border collie standard.

It is my great hope that our breed is not spoilt by ear judges. Even at this early stage there are judges who look and place dogs only when they have tipped ears, regardless of the rest of the dog. If this happens too often, it could well result in the ruination of the breed.

Crufts 1984 was judged by Bill Dixon. We did not enter our dogs but we

*Show Champion
Huntroyde Beau Brummel
at Sanrian.*

were very interested to read that the Kilsbys' Show Champion Tork of
Whenway again won the challenge certificate. The best of breed ticket went
to Gina Croft's Melodor Flurry of Falconmoor, now a show champion, who
went on to win reserve best in the group under Joe Braddon.

Mrs Marion Leigh Hopkinson judged the breed at Crufts 1985. Marion
was one of those instrumental in the acceptance of the border collie on to the
Kennel Club register, so it was fitting that she should be asked to judge at
this most prestigious show. Her dog challenge certificate winner was Mr and
Mrs Goddard's Huntroyde Beau Brummel at Sanrian, now a show
champion, with the reserve challenge certificate going to Bruce Kilsby's
Show Champion Tork of Whenway. Obviously a very lucky show for the
Kilsbys and Tork. The bitch ticket went to Show Champion Tracelyn Gal,
owned and handled by Eric Broadhurst. The reserve ticket was won by Miss
Mill's Mizanne the Lady Lucinda, daughter of Show Champion Mizanne
the Witch, who won the bitch ticket at Crufts in 1983, when I judged.

In 1987 the breed were allocated twenty sets of tickets. We can now
compete for challenge certificates at Crufts, Bath, Birmingham, National
Scottish Kennel Club, Southern Counties Association, Three Counties,
Border Union, Windsor, East of England, Leeds, Bournemouth, Welsh

Kennel Club, Darlington Midland Counties, Ladies Kennel Association, National Working Breeds, Working Breeds of Scotland, Working Breeds of Wales, and both the Border Collie Club of Great Britain, and the Southern Border Collie Club. In 1988 the Northern Border Collie Club will have tickets as well. All these championship shows will need either specialist or all round judges to officiate. There are a few specialist judges with the necessary years of experience of judging behind them but it will mean many more all round judges will be given the opportunity to judge the breed. Let us sincerely hope that they have an interest in the breed, and will not just accept the judging appointment so that they can add another breed to the list of challenge certificates that they can give.

One can't help but wonder at the variety of types when looking at the large entry of border collies at the shows now. Judges that have no interest or knowledge of the breed could do untold damage to the future show dogs by placing untypical, poor specimens. There are those judges who look for animation, regardless of the other important points. It is true we want our dogs to show normal liveliness, they are well known for showing interest in everything. But wildness should not be mistaken for liveliness. There are still too many untrained borders, some it could be said, showing viscious tendencies. By the time the border reaches the championship show ring he should have had some small amount of training so that the reputation for being crazy, uncontrolled animals can be denied. No one expects the dogs to stand like statues, with a dead pan expression, and there is no need for them to curb their natural alertness.

A clever breed like the border collie can be trained to show suppressed excitement and a certain amount of animation, and still stand correctly, ready for inspection by the judge. There are some well behaved and properly show-trained borders, and their reward is to be placed in the winning line up, where they can show off their other good points such as construction and type to the best advantage. With all the other attributes requested by the standard, good behaviour for the judge's assessment usually swings the decision for the top placing in their favour. Judges do not have the time to chase the dog around and wait for it to stand still before going over it, imagine the time wasted if all were so active and untrained.

There are also judges who only look for and place the popular and evenly marked black and white dogs and bitches. Sadly, it can be noticed that dogs with nothing more than the white blaze, collar, four white feet, tail tip and chest in their favour, get placed regularly in the winning line up. There are many border collies with excellent construction and super movement who do not have the classic white markings and are overlooked. I admit that even markings help the picture, a white leg and unevenly marked black leg gives the impression that the dog comes towards you out at elbow on the side where the black leg is. The judge has to take all these factors into account and those knowing the breed will make allowances. But those with scanty knowledge will make judging the border collie a chore rather than a pleasure.

The Southern Border Collie Club has organised judging seminars and it is to the club's credit that they are doing something about educating the future judges. I served on the judging panel and watched the would-be newcomers attempting the most difficult task of the dog game. It was a very interesting education. Some approached the task with trepidation, nervously going over each dog in front of them and whispering their requests to the exhibitors. When making their final assessment for the placing, they stood gazing at the dogs unable to make up their minds which dog should be placed first, or even which order any of the dogs should be placed. In some cases, these were exhibitors who had done a good bit of winning themselves. But because a person is a good handler with good dogs and attends shows regularly, it does not follow that they can judge. Judges are born, no amount of training, classes, or lessons can make a judge. The judges in days gone by learnt their trade by experience aided by the the gift of an eye for a good dog.

The Judging Procedure: I assess and compare each dog that has assembled in the ring prior to going over individual dogs. By standing well back from the dog, the whole picture can be seen.

Always approach the dog from the front, there must be no nervous backing away. This was the eventual challenge certificate and best of breed winner Mrs Pat Haydock's Show Champion Wizaland Jake of Eyot.

First thing that is gone over is the head. I am holding the head firmly and assessing eye colour, pigment, expression and length of muzzle to skull.

Skull must be horizontal to muzzle with stop halfway. There must be no drop away of underjaw. By placing the hand flat on the skull, and looking sideways at the head, I can see horizontal plane, and if there is enough underjaw.

I stand behind dog to check shoulder angulation. From this angle I can assess correct length of neck, and whether shoulders are well laid back.

I feel for depth of brisket, and correct lay of ribs, which must be well sprung.

I check for level and strong topline.

I feel for length of ribcage which must be three quarters of body, and correct length of loin.

Standing behind dog, I feel for loose elbows. Elbows must be held close to the body. I assess all over outline, especially bend of stifle and correct height of hocks, hindquarters strong with good set on of tail.

The dog is moving away so I can assess correct action from rear. On the return I check that the dog is not pin-toeing with elbows wider than paws on the move.

I check that the dog is entire, and the hindquarters have good muscle.

Also on the move, I check that the dog is holding his topline with no dip behind the withers.

The dog has been picked as a second prize winner of a class and I am writing a quick summary of the dog's good points, and noting any bad points. This particular dog is Mrs Pat Wilkinson's Altricia Merc.

All dogs were being judged outside at Windsor Championship Show. The lightning thunder and heavy rain kept the exhibitors and judge inside for the bitch judging. All Championship Show organisers provide large tents for wet weather accommodation. This is the line up for the junior bitch class. First was Mrs Judith Gregory's Tonkory Eliza, second was Mrs Angela Gillespie's Detania Giglet, third was Mrs Pat Wilkinson's Altricia Mercedes, reserve was Mrs Kidd's Caristan Belle Star at Cookaby, and very highly commended was Mrs Goodwin's Viber California Girl.

The trainees who had previous judging experience with other breeds, were not so nervous. They took command of the ring as they entered and they made their requests with authority. This gains the respect of the exhibitors, who like to know that the judge knows what he wants and has the experience and knowledge to take command of the ring where he is judging.

We have watched some of the all round judges who seem amazed at the huge entries of border collies as they come into the show ring, all types, colours and sizes. They must think that this is a breed in the very early stages of type development. In fact, it is the only breed that has been accepted by the Kennel Club for show in recent times that has increased so dramatically in numbers in the show ring. The answer is, of course, that the breed was already well established with the International Sheepdog Society and members jumped at the chance to show their dogs by registering with the Kennel Club. There was no need to import stock with the added expense of quarantine bills, the border collie was already here in the British Isles.

Judging the border collie at the present time is a most rewarding occupation. It is a challenge. The specialist judges have no wish to alter the breed in any way. They liked what they saw way back in 1976 and they wish to continue with their breeding programme, sticking strictly to what the

Challenge certificate winning bitch at Windsor – Tony Holliday's Ruscombe Astra at Corinlea, now a show champion.

early shepherds have bred for generations. The specialist judge will look for soundness in construction, balance and that super movement only the border can portray when perfectly made. Most of the specialist judges are also breeders and this extra knowledge means that they will keep the border collie as it always has been. Because they choose to exhibit their dogs in the beauty ring and also accept judging appointments, shows how much they appreciate this versatile breed and wish to take it into another field of sport.

CHAPTER NINE

Judging Lists

THE Kennel Club expect all clubs to compile judging lists, these usually consist of specialist judges who are passed to give challenge certificates in the breed and comply with the club's qualifications. The judges list is also compiled of names of all round judges who give challenge certificates in several different breeds. The A list includes those who can judge groups and best in show at championship shows.

The B list is usually comprised of candidates, who in the opinion of the club that is issuing the list, are qualified to give challenge certificates but have not been approved by the Kennel Club. From this list clubs usually pick their open and limited show judges.

List C is comprised of candidates who have qualifications but not enough to go on the B List. They are usually asked to judge limited and sanction shows. These are often people who have owned the breed, for a few years and have shown an interest in the judging procedure.

Specialists are in great demand to judge breed club shows, the exhibitors believe that they are more familiar with the breed and can assess the dogs with more knowledge. Personally, we like to show under specialists and all-round judges. If we find the judge on the day does not like our type of dog, we might give him one more chance. If we receive the same result, we then cross that judge's name from our list. It is noticeable that specialist judges seem to judge very much to the type that they breed or own, and regular showgoers soon get to know which judges like their dogs and which judges have a completely different idea on what type they will place in the winning line-up.

The all round judge might have owned several different breeds in the past and though he is unlikely to have owned all the breeds that he can give challenge certificates to, he will have developed a trained eye for a good dog. These judges will usually have done their homework and with their experience they will be able to assess the good and bad points of the dog in front of them. They could also have judged many of the breeds in the variety classes that are classified at all the open shows. In those classes some real top dogs are entered.

It is rather a shame that so many breed clubs prefer to have specialist judges on their lists, and only one or two all round judges. The specialist seem to pin-point their assessment on one or two favourable points like tail set, or ear carriage, and do not take into account the whole dog. The all rounder looks at the complete picture when choosing his winners, and bears in mind his interpretation of the standard and picks out that type.

Suggestions for Judging List Qualifications

LIST A: Candidates must have awarded Kennel Club challenge certificates in the breed.

LIST B: This list is comprised of candidates who in the opinion of the breed club are qualified to give challenge certificates but as yet have not been approved by the Kennel Club. Candidates must fulfil No. 1 and at least (3) of the qualifications listed below:-

    1. Have judged 40 classes of the breed at open show level.

    2. Have been on a breed club open show list for at least three years.

    3. Have owned the breed for at least ten years.

    4. Have exhibited or judged the breed within the last two years.

    5. Have bred or qualified either one of the breed or two individual challenge certificate winners, or qualified five for entry into the Kennel Club stud book.

    6. Have awarded challenge certificates in at least one other breed.

LIST C: This list is comprised of candidates for sanction, limit and open show list. Candidates must fulfil No. 1 and at least one other of the qualifications.

    1. Have judged at least 15 classes of the breed with a minimum of 90 dogs at open show level or have judged 10 classes of the breed with a minimum of 60 dogs at open show level, plus 10 classes with a minimum of 60 dogs of another working breed at open show level.

    2. Have owned or handled regularly the breed for at least five years.

    3. Have qualified two of the breed for entry into the Kennel Club Stud Book.

    4. Be on the open show judging list of at least one other breed club.

Line Breeding

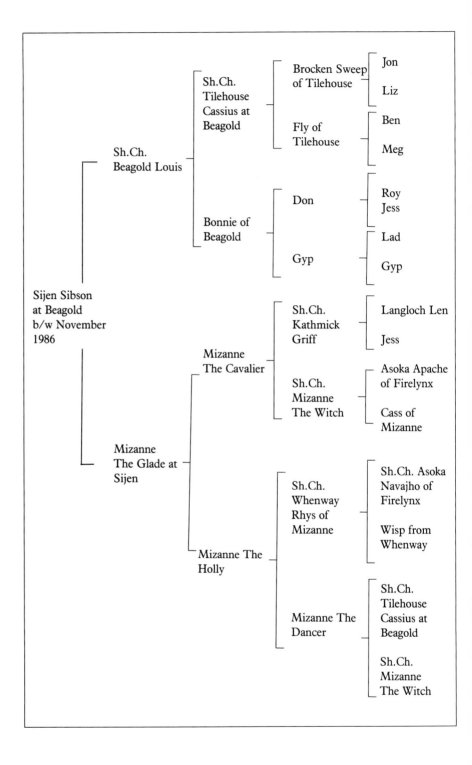

CHAPTER TEN

Breeding

IT is not long after a border collie owner starts winning in the show ring that they have the first thoughts about producing a litter from their bitch or having another dog puppy sired by their winning dog. They could just go out and buy another dog or bitch, but there is a great temptation among enthusiasts to breed their own litter.

If they have read, learned and studied well, they could be in line for success. But on the other hand, there are many who rush their bitch along to the dog that is in winning form with no thought of what might be produced in the resulting litter. I have often heard of border collie owners who are proud to mention that a particular dog is way back in their bitch's pedigree and when they choose the stud for their bitch, they keep a special look out for that dog's name. Much more study is needed, and in years to come there will be breeders who have never even heard of the excellent working dogs featured strongly in today's pedigrees. In fact, the faults that show up from generation to generation will, no doubt, be blamed on those famous working dogs.

METHOD OF BREEDING
When the aim is to produce show worthy border collies from quality dogs, certain points should be observed so both parents of the proposed union are compatible in type, health, temperament, soundness and character.

LINE BREEDING
This is the mating of grandson to grand-dam, grandsire to grand-daughter, nephew to aunt, uncle to neice, and cousin to cousin. Similar characteristics will be produced in the resulting litter from the dominant ancestors, so it is important that type and temperament, soundness and health are what you are aiming to produce. Less desirable features will also be present, inherited from hidden faults unknown in the strain so it is doubly important to use pure stock.

Mrs Jenifer Garner discussed with us the most suitable dog to use on her bitch Mizanne The Glade of Sijen. The Glade was not well boned and needed more substance. She had an excellent line bred pedigree but needed a stronger line to correct the one or two faults she had for show. We suggested that she should line breed by using Show Champion Beagold Louis. He had good bone, excellent front and rear and a low set tail which he carried down. He also had a good head and length of neck and had sired puppies with good substance, very similar to himself. His coat was of good texture with a thick undercoat. His temperament was excellent. In fact Louis's sire was Show Champion Tilehouse Cassius at Beagold a very calm dog, and Louis's dam was also a calm bitch.

We had a dog puppy from the litter and he inherited a lot of good points from his sire, mainly a good outline, excellent front and rear, good coat, long tail that he carried low and good ear set. He also inherited the very lively, active temperament with strong working instinct from his great grandsire Show Champion Kathmick Griff. His great great grandsire was Show Champion Tilehouse Cassius at Beagold and his great great grand-dam was Show Champion Mizanne The Witch. The puppy was called Sijen Sibson at Beagold and he is one of the few show border collies to be fifth generation show border collie stock.

IN-BREEDING

This is when sire is mated to daughter, son to dam, brother to sister. This close breeding is really only for the expert breeder to tackle. These unions will establish strong desirable good points that appear in both parents, but it will also cement the bad points to such a degree that it will be hard to eradicate for many generations to come.

Hours of study should be undertaken before any in-breeding on a breed such as the border collie. The breed is so new to the show world, all that we have gleaned is from International Sheepdog Society information catering for the working capabilities of the breed. Novices would do well to attempt line breeding at the present time, and only in-breed if they are willing to cull or sell as pets without papers any of the resulting litter that do not meet with the show requirements.

The pedigree of Guigan at Beagold shows how we have tried to bring in the strong good points of Bonnie of Beagold the dam of Guigan who is also the dam of Beagold Marvelous Marvin – the sire. The grand-dam of Guigan is also the dam of Guigan – a mother-son mating. In fact, it was successful in many respects. Guigan had a strong excellent shaped head, super straight good textured coat with a good undercoat, good bone, good length of neck, dark eyes, beautifully high set tipped ears. He had good tail set and carriage and excellent forequarters.

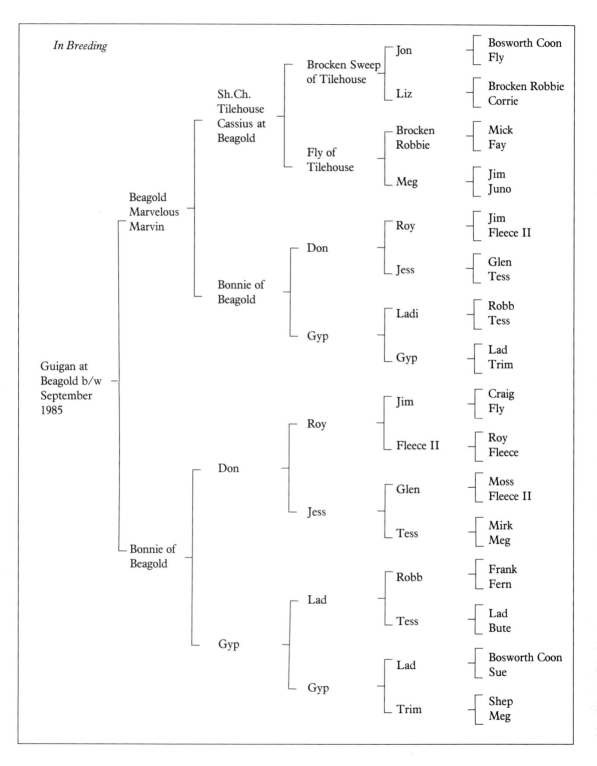

Guigan at Beagold

Marvin did not have as good hindquarters as we would have liked and with all the excellent points in the combination breeding, the only slight fault that Guigan inherited was a slight weakness in rear action. This meant that extra free running exercise was needed to strengthen his hind muscles and plenty of steady road walking on the lead so that he developed a smoother gait. Bonnie's rear actions was excellent, so the problem must have come from another direction.

By using Guigan at stud we must be careful to eliminate that weakness so he must use a bitch with very strong hindquarters. We do not need to strengthen temperament or character as he is gifted with perfect temperament and excellent character. Ron Saunders, the breeder of Guigan, discussed the possibility of mating mother to son in this breeding. We were completely in agreement because as far as we knew there were no abnormalities in either parent and we were interested to see the results.

COLOUR BREEDING
This is a specialist form of breeding where the emphasis is on producing one particular characteristic – that is colour. Breeder Mrs Sue Ader was very

Colour Breeding

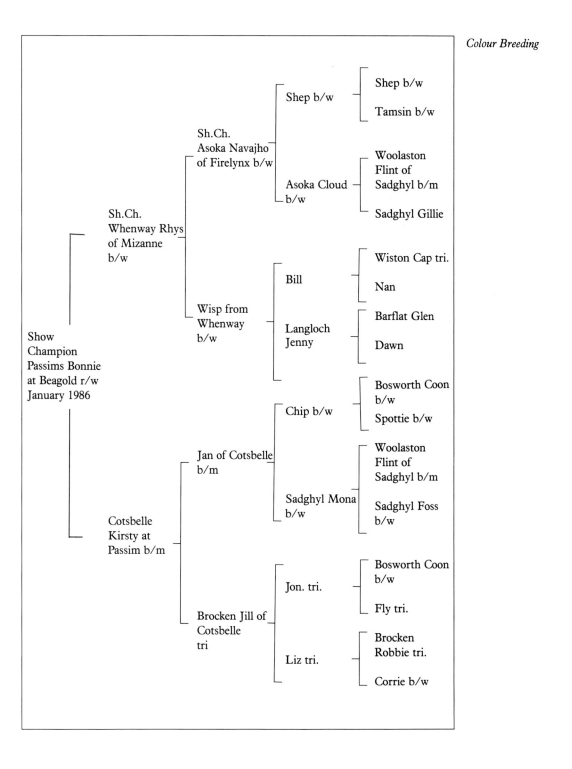

Show Champion Passims Bonnie at Beagold r/w January 1986

- Sh.Ch. Whenway Rhys of Mizanne b/w
  - Sh.Ch. Asoka Navajho of Firelynx b/w
    - Shep b/w
      - Shep b/w
      - Tamsin b/w
    - Asoka Cloud b/w
      - Woolaston Flint of Sadghyl b/m
      - Sadghyl Gillie
  - Wisp from Whenway b/w
    - Bill
      - Wiston Cap tri.
      - Nan
    - Langloch Jenny
      - Barflat Glen
      - Dawn
- Cotsbelle Kirsty at Passim b/m
  - Jan of Cotsbelle b/m
    - Chip b/w
      - Bosworth Coon b/w
      - Spottie b/w
    - Sadghyl Mona b/w
      - Woolaston Flint of Sadghyl b/m
      - Sadghyl Foss b/w
  - Brocken Jill of Cotsbelle tri
    - Jon. tri.
      - Bosworth Coon b/w
      - Fly tri.
    - Liz tri.
      - Brocken Robbie tri.
      - Corrie b/w

Blue merle bitch Daisy Belle of Jaybank.

Colhurst Ruby Red. The first red merle to win a challenge certificate

*Show Champion
Passims Bonnie
at Beagold.*

interested in producing colours other than black and white in her breeding, never forgetting the overall type as well. Blue merle is on both sides of the pedigree of Show Champion Passims Bonnie at Beagold, who is red and white in colour. The only tan colour mentioned is in the tri-coloured border collies. If there were tan or red coloured puppies in the litter of the dogs mentioned, there is no way of knowing. It is obvious from this pedigree that blue merle and tri-colour on both sides of the pedigree is a good indication that mixed colours will appear strongly in each litter. It is a well known fact that Passims Bonnie's sire Show Champion Whenway Rhys of Mizanne has produced red/white puppies to different bitches. Also the Sadghyl breeding is very strong for blue merle. Mrs Ader has chosen as her foundation bitch the blue merle Cotsbelle Kirsty at Passim.

OUT-CROSSING
When the border collie was first accepted for show, the breeders had no choice but to out-cross. In the past the International Sheepdog Society (ISDS) registered dogs and bitches were bred for their working capabilities and not for their looks. Although no one wanted the breed to lose any of its original character, there were certain points that were needed for a show dog

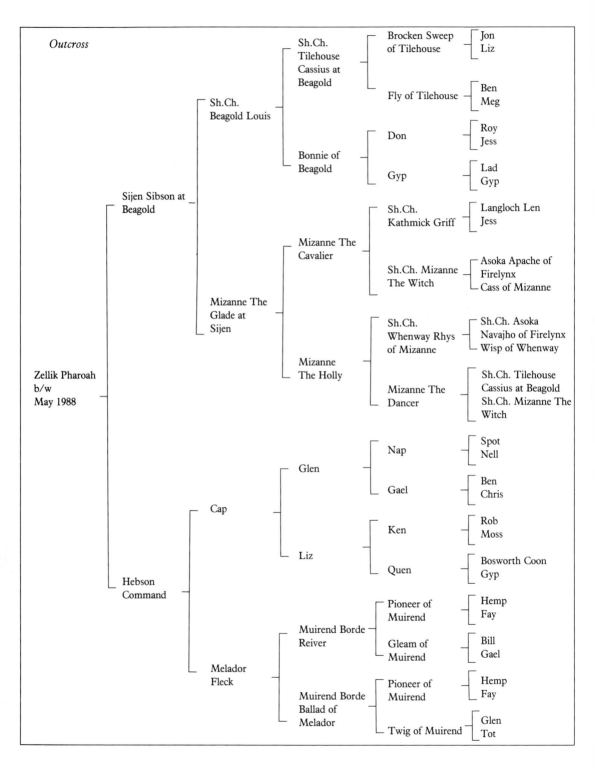

Outcross

Zellik Pharoah
b/w
May 1988

*Obedience champion
Whenway Mist of
Wizaland. Winner of
three obedience challenge
certificates and one breed
challenge certificate*

*David Bull, Our Dogs
photographer*

and only careful selection would produce that requirement.

There were many well constructed good quality ISDS registered dogs to choose from. But breeders had to take careful notes from the litters so they did not double up on construction faults. If a dog could not work for the farmer it was not kept so any weakness that a dog and bitch produced was immediately culled. But that did not mean the fault was eliminated from the line. Another dog used on the faulty bitch might well carry a recessive gene that would only show up in the offspring. A faulty dog carrying a recessive gene fault could pass it on for several generations. That is what we have to guard against when we are choosing a mate for our dog or bitch. Only after two or three litters can we say for sure that our line is clear of any noticeable faults in construction or temperament.

We very rarely out-crossed in our bearded collie breeding once we had produced several generations of sound stock we line bred and in-bred to establish a strong type. Colour is not a major factor in our choice of a breeding couple. Our main aim is to produce a well constructed good type border collie, with clear markings. Right at the bottom of our requirements, comes colour and we would be quite happy to produce a red-white dog if it conformed to our overall breed type.

Show Champion
Wizaland Jake of Eyot.

Wizaland McIntosh by Show Champion Tork of Whenway out of Whenway Mist of Wizaland. Winner of one challenge certificate and one reserve challenge certificate.

David Bull, Our Dogs photographer

However tempting it is to go to a handsome well constructed working dog, we always play safe by using the dogs that have proved to us for several generations that there are no hidden problems that might arise in our breeding. We prefer to arrive at our idea of a perfect border collie slowly, rather than look for quick results that might never materialise.

Mr and Mrs Kilsby mated the slight feminine bitch Andersley Demelza from Whenway to the strongly made big boned Gelert of Gawne from Whenway. They gave the bitch Whenway Mist of Wizaland to Mrs Sue Large, who made her an obedience champion. Mrs Large then took the bitch to Mr and Mrs Kilsby's Show Champion Tork of Whenway twice. In the first litter was Wizaland McIntosh and Wizaland Jake of Eyot. McIntosh has won a challenge certificate and reserve challenge certificate. Jake is now a show champion.

The large bone and size in the breeding comes from the grandsire on both sides. It is watered down in some of the descendants by the finer feminine bitches. Both Tork and his son Wizaland Jake produce quality and correct size when mated to bitches that come from middle of the road size ancestors.

	SIRE	GRANDSIRE
		Clun Roy
	Sh.Ch. Tork of Whenway.	
Sh.Ch. Wizaland Jake of Eyot. and Wizaland McIntosh		Belle Gelert of Gawne from Whenway
	Ob.Ch. Whenway Mist of Wizaland.	
		Andersley Demelza from Whenway.

It is noticeable that most breeders currently seem to be out-crossing and chancing what they get in each litter. The variety of types in the show ring offers an excellent opportunity to pick and choose a stud dog, if breeders are willing to take pot luck on the resulting litter. Those who wish to establish a type, the temperament and character of what they believe to be the true border collie, work more carefully. They spend time extending their knowledge of the breed before choosing their foundation stock. The clever breeder will plan and research if they wish to fix their own strain, so that only the purist lines and true types come through on their future stock. They are aiming for border collies that will immediately be recognised as dogs bred by

Father and son Show Champion Tilehouse Cassius at Beagold with Henhamfield Risk Me At Beagold pictured at seven weeks.

Kelly sired by Show Champion Beagold Louis out of Viber Lovers Tiff.

Mizanne The Dancer
(Show Champion
Tilehouse Cassius at
Beagold – Mizanne The
Witch).

their kennel carrying their prefix.

A variety of types will continue to win in the show ring for some time yet. But it would be unwise to use a particular dog at stud because of his show wins. Much more study is needed to find out the real worth of the dog, what stock he has produced and if he was the only one in the litter that had the temperament and requirements that can be seen in him. A good looking dog does not necessarily produce good looking puppies.

CHAPTER ELEVEN

The Stud Dog

The border collie that is chosen as a stud dog must answer all the requirements of the Breed Standard such as conformation, type and soundness. I interpret this as:

Conformation: Well shaped head, good length of neck on to withers, then level top line sloping gently over croup, low set tail well feathered. Correct length of rib cage, not too long in the loin. Good bend of stifle, muscled and not too low on hock. Feathering in the usual places, nice tight feet well knuckled. Strong but not coarse bone. Slight waves, but not a curly coat. A gleaming healthy looking textured coat shows up in a top quality stud dog.

Type: The dog you choose must be immediately recognisable as a border collie with unmistakable characteristics of the breed so that the resulting progeny will give the same immediate impression.

Soundness: Free from any deformity or sickness that might be past on to his offspring. Collie eye anomaly and progressive retinal atrophy should be tested for clearance and a clearance certificate for hip displasia should be obtained from the British Veterinary Association.

If the dog is worth breeding from then he must not only look good in stance, he must also move correctly. First class movement is a result of good conformation and that is passed on to the dog's progeny. It is a well known fact that a pair of champions, perfect in many respects, could easily produce offspring utterly devoid of the virtues of their parents. It is always a gamble when attempting any form of breeding. But two quality dogs have a much better chance of producing something good, than two faulty animals. A stud dog that is shelly and light boned, in spite of being reared correctly, will produce a large proportion of his progeny with the same faulty characteristics. It is the stud dog that has produced his like in several litters with this prepotency showing in large numbers of his winning offspring, even to a variety of indifferent bitches, that will be in great demand. Poor quality bitches should not be bred from. No stud dog, even the greatest, can correct all the faults.

Temperament is a most important consideration in border collies. By their nature they are expected to be alert, bold and courageous guard dogs. Strict discipline tempered with love and kindness will help channel the over boldness that you might find in some dogs and bitches, into the correct behaviour. Bad temperament can be inherited or acquired. Any dog that displays over aggressiveness or is a fear-biter, should never be bred from. A sweet tempered animal that has been treated badly, can turn aggressive. A dog that has been deprived of human companionship or teased continually by children, can retaliate in the only way it knows how.

When there has been an opportunity to see the stud dog's offspring in the show ring, then the choice is an easy one. Although it is still not the main aim of most border collie breeders to choose dogs for their good looks or show wins. They are not even predisposed to use a stud dog that is consistently producing show winning puppies. So many of the breeders are keen to keep the working instinct and the working capabilities in the breed so they use a dog that has all these characteristics in preference to the show dog. I believe that the top show dogs, at this stage in the show development of the breed, are only one or two generations away from working parents, so good looks go hand in hand with the capabilities for work. But not all border collies bred on farms from generation to generation of working ancestors have the keeness to work sheep. It is also important to bear in mind that the puppies we breed are very unlikely to encounter sheep, so there is no real need to retain their strong working instinct. Breeding in a strong working instinct could only produce frustration and consequently other temperamental problems.

We have built up a small record in pictures and pedigrees of dogs that feature in our stock's pedigrees and this is invaluable when planning a breeding programme. By studying the photographs of the ancestors of our dogs and bitches we obtain a good idea of the type of puppy that will result from certain combinations when mated together. Photographs are useful when there is no possibility of seeing the real thing. Large championship shows are the places to go it you want to see show champions and these are the dogs that are quite often used at stud. The dogs that are chosen purely for their working capabilities are not often shown in the show ring. Their construction and looks are considered, but only secondary to their reputation as a worker.

The mistake the novice breeder could make is not knowing the type, looks and construction of the stud dog's littermates. He could well be a good looking dog but his brothers and sisters could be of a poorer quality type. The faults will then be passed on to the resulting litter, as the influence of the stud dog is the major factor and he will be carrying the genes from his parents. Some breeders will not use a tri-colour dog at stud, preferring to minimise the chance of producing tri-colour puppies in their litter, a colour not so popular as black and white. The judges seem to favour the black and white exhibits. Blue merle, red merle, red and white and the smooth coated border collie stud dog would be used very seldom, if at all, although recently there has been an interest shown in these colours. A mis-marked stud dog, with a majority of white rather than black, would certainly sire mis-marked puppies in the litters. There are one or two currently being shown with patchy white markings on the black but they are not considered too often for top awards by the judges who are looking for the classic markings.

The stud dog must be kept healthy and in tip-top condition at all times. He must be ready to accept bitches that come for mating even if they are aggressive, he also must be willing to accept his owner holding the bitch if it is needed. Only a willing and keen stud dog should be advertised at stud. No one wants to travel a long distance to be confronted with a timid and reluctant stud dog. That is why we keep our dogs away from our bitches. A trained stud dog would worry himself thin and completely out of condition if he was allowed to run with bitches in season. In fact, he would know that they were coming into season before they have a colour discharge. The bitch would snap and growl at him for days before she would allow him to mate

Brocken Sweep of Tilehouse: sire of Show Champion Tilehouse Cassius at Beagold.

Fly of Tilehouse: dam of Cassius.

David Dalton ▼   ▲ *Diane Pearce*

Show Champion Tilehouse Cassius at Beagold.

her. Then, if he was the chosen stud for that particular bitch, he would have worn himself out by the time he was encouraged to mount her. It is not always wise to use your own stud dog, certainly not at every season. Also, if the pair are close relations and you have not planned an in-breeding programme, you risk doubling up on noticeable faults.

If possible, we like to keep two or three stud dogs of each breed that we own. When a bitch comes to be mated we do not make an automatic choice. We like to assess each animal's merits and its bad points. We never choose a stud dog that has the same undesirable faults as the bitch, but whenever possible we like to double up on the good points. Temperament is of the greatest importance. To mate a wild, active, outgoing dog to a similar tempered bitch might be ideal for some purposes but if the majority of puppies are going to pet homes, it would be a foolish decision.

We like to prove our young dogs first with our own bitches. We would choose a quiet bitch, usually older than the dog that has been used for breeding before. She will accept the dog and encourage his advances, without turning aggressive. If in doubt, muzzle the bitch. A vicious bad temper display from a maiden bitch, which is quite usual behaviour, might

Hebson Craig, stud dog owned by Pat Jones.

put a young stud dog off mating for life. When trained, the dog will sniff and lick the bitch, then mount her, making several thrusts until he achieves a 'tie'. We hold him on her back for several minutes so that his enlarged penis is tightly held by the bitch. Then we help him to move off her back and they are then quite comfortable standing back to back during the 'tie'. We never allow the dog or bitch to pull each other around or to snap at each other. We never leave them to their own devices. Our stud dogs have such confidence in us that they even shut their eyes and rest their heads on our laps while they are in this position.

There are so many people who say that the pair should be left to their own devices, it should be a natural mating, as in the wild state. But they are not in the wild. They are domesticated animals in a completely different situation so we believe that any help we can give for their comfort and safety is necessary.

The 'tie' can last a few minutes or up to an hour. If the bitch has been brought at the correct time, not too early or too late, there should be a litter born in about sixty three days. We do not allow our dogs to mate bitches more than once a week. We suggest to the bitch's owner that the bitch should be brought again for a second mating with one day in between, so that if the first day is too early, the second day could well be spot on. Our dogs are always ready and more than willing to accept the bitch the second time. After the mating we wash our dog well with disinfectant and return him to rest in his own kennel. We never allow a dog that has just mated a bitch to mix with other dogs, they could well react aggressively.

Whenever possible, we like to view the resulting litter when the puppies are about six weeks. Then we can assess the quality of the litter and take notice if our stud dog's prepotency has dominated the litter. Sometimes we agree to take a puppy in lieu of stud fee if we like the look of the bitch and her pedigree ties in with our own borders. Then it is even more important to assess the quality of the litter at six weeks of age so that we can see if it is our dog that is the dominant factor, producing his like to the line bred or in-bred bitch that he mated.

If possible, we only accept bitches for our stud dogs that will be brought by the owners and taken away after service. Very few bitches settle in happily in a strange kennel after such a traumatic experience. Should a bitch miss having puppies after the correct time, we offer a free stud service at her next season. There could be a number of reasons why she did not conceive. But if she misses again, we suggest that the vet should be consulted, especially if our stud dog has mated bitches with success in the interim period.

CHAPTER TWELVE

The Brood Bitch

WE have found that border collie bitches make excellent mothers. The first border litter that we bred was from Destiny by Moss. Destiny was not due to whelp until I had returned from a judging appointment abroad, giving plenty of time to take her from her kennel into the warm whelping room. We arrived home from America in bitter cold weather, with snow on the ground, to find that Destiny had whelped four puppies, more than a week before her time. She had kept them warm and attended to herself with no problem in her outside kennel.

We wrapped the puppies in a blanket and brought them into the whelping room, where Destiny settled down again to have three more pups. No bother or fuss, and this was her first litter. She attended to each puppy herself, cleaning them every minute, and covered them with paper bedding when she left them. With such perfect attention they soon became fat, healthy little pups. Then quite happily she gave up her maternal duties and returned to her own kennel without a backward glance when the pups were six weeks old. Destiny was over two when she was first mated, and this seems to be the best time when a bitch is mature and able to cope satisfactorily with the trials of motherhood.

We once visited a border collie breeder in Germany and when we arrived he was busy phoning around for a foster mother for the six pups his bitch had just whelped and would not accept. The bitch was over five years old and this was her first litter. The breeder was afraid she would hurt the pups and had put her back in her outside kennel, leaving the pups in a warm room on their own. He had tried for several hours to persuade the bitch to suckle, but she had rejected the pups every time. I asked if I could try to help, as I had encountered similar problems with different breeds.

The bitch was brought back into the room and gently but firmly, we made her lie down. Still holding her head, we put each puppy to her nipples. All the while we gently massaged the teats so that the milk came down. She fought and had to be forcibly held but one by one the puppies were able to suck. We have found that some bitches experience genuine shock when they first give birth. They need plenty of understanding to encourage them to accept their puppies. This applies particularly to the bitch that has been a loner all her life and has always prefered her own company to that of other dogs. Suddenly she is surrounded by squirming, crying creatures, making demands on her – and they bear no resemblance to anything she has encountered in the past. If a bitch has reached the age of five years without a litter she has tremendous adjustments to make, yet she has no natural maternal instincts to fall back on. Once the puppies can be persuaded to suckle and the milk comes down into the teats the bitch will accept them, as this one did. Later, we went into the room to check her and she growled, warning us to leave her and her family alone.

It is therefore generally desirable to mate a bitch when she is around two years old. As soon as the bitch comes into season, the owner of the stud dog should be contacted so that the dog is kept in readiness. It is so difficult to say for certain when is the correct day to mate any particular bitch. Some produce puppies after being mated at the seventh day, others are successful in producing litters when mated as late as the twentieth day. Usually the pundits say from the eleventh to the thirteenth day. We prefer to check our bitch daily and when the colour of the discharge changes to a sticky pinkish colour we mate for the first time that day. We then leave a day and mate again the next. Another sign is that the vulva is swollen and soft. There seems to be no hard and fast rule, we have had bitches produce litters after being mated on the seventh day, and have also had a litter from bitches mated on the twentieth day. We have also been unsuccessful when the bitch was mated at the supposedly correct time.

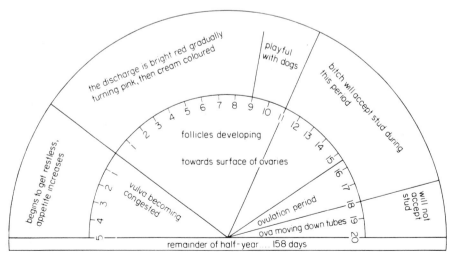

Chart showing the mating cycle of a normal bitch.

Table showing when a bitch is due to whelp.

Served Jan.	Whelps March	Served Feb.	Whelps April	Served March	Whelps May	Served April	Whelps June	Served May	Whelps July	Served June	Whelps Aug.	Served July	Whelps Sept.	Served Aug.	Whelps Oct.	Served Sept.	Whelps Nov.	Served Oct.	Whelps Dec.	Served Nov.	Whelps Jan.	Served Dec.	Whelps Feb.
1	5	1	5	1	3	1	3	1	3	1	3	1	2	1	3	1	3	1	3	1	3	1	2
2	6	2	6	2	4	2	4	2	4	2	4	2	3	2	4	2	4	2	4	2	4	2	3
3	7	3	7	3	5	3	5	3	5	3	5	3	4	3	5	3	5	3	5	3	5	3	4
4	8	4	8	4	6	4	6	4	6	4	6	4	5	4	6	4	6	4	6	4	6	4	5
5	9	5	9	5	7	5	7	5	7	5	7	5	6	5	7	5	7	5	7	5	7	5	6
6	10	6	10	6	8	6	8	6	8	6	8	6	7	6	8	6	8	6	8	6	8	6	7
7	11	7	11	7	9	7	9	7	9	7	9	7	8	7	9	7	9	7	9	7	9	7	8
8	12	8	12	8	10	8	10	8	10	8	10	8	9	8	10	8	10	8	10	8	10	8	9
9	13	9	13	9	11	9	11	9	11	9	11	9	10	9	11	9	11	9	11	9	11	9	10
10	14	10	14	10	12	10	12	10	12	10	12	10	11	10	12	10	12	10	12	10	12	10	11
11	15	12	15	11	13	11	13	11	13	11	13	11	12	11	13	11	13	11	13	11	13	11	12
12	16	13	16	12	14	12	14	12	14	12	14	12	13	12	14	12	14	12	14	12	14	12	13
13	17	14	17	13	15	13	15	13	15	13	15	13	14	13	15	13	15	13	15	13	15	13	14
14	18	15	18	14	16	14	16	14	16	14	16	14	15	14	16	14	16	14	16	14	16	14	15
15	19	16	19	15	17	15	17	15	17	15	17	15	16	15	17	15	17	15	17	15	17	15	16
16	20	17	20	16	18	16	18	16	18	16	18	16	17	16	18	16	18	16	18	16	18	16	17
17	21	18	21	17	19	17	19	17	19	17	19	17	18	17	19	17	19	17	19	17	19	17	18
18	22	19	22	18	20	18	20	18	20	18	20	18	19	18	20	18	20	18	20	18	20	18	19
19	23	20	23	19	21	19	21	19	21	19	21	19	20	19	21	19	21	19	21	19	21	19	20
20	24	21	24	20	22	20	22	20	22	20	22	20	21	20	22	20	22	20	22	20	22	20	21
21	25	22	25	21	23	21	23	21	23	21	23	21	22	21	23	21	23	21	23	21	23	21	22
22	26	23	26	22	24	22	24	22	24	22	24	22	23	22	24	22	24	22	24	22	24	22	23
23	27	24	27	23	25	23	25	23	25	23	25	23	24	23	25	23	25	23	25	23	25	23	24
24	28	25	28	24	26	24	26	24	26	24	26	24	25	24	26	24	26	24	26	24	26	24	25
25	29	26	29	25	27	25	27	25	27	25	27	25	26	25	27	25	27	25	27	25	27	25	26
26	30	27	30	26	28	26	28	26	28	26	28	26	27	26	28	26	28	26	28	26	28	26	27
27	31	28	1	27	29	27	29	27	29	27	29	27	28	27	29	27	29	27	29	27	29	27	28
28	1	29	2	28	30	28	30	28	30	28	30	28	29	28	30	28	30	28	30	28	30	28	1
29	2			29	31	29	1	29	31	29	31	29	30	29	31	29	1	29	31	29	31	29	2
30	3			30	1	30	2	30	1	30	1	30	1	30	1	30	2	30	1	30	1	30	3
31	4			31	2			31	2			31	2	31	2			31	2			31	4

We once had a bitch that came to be mated and when I checked her, she had an infection of the vulva. We refused to allow the mating and suggested the owner took the bitch straight to the vet. She was brought back on the thirteenth day after the vet put her on a course of antibiotics. We had a telephone call ten days later to say that the owner's own dog had broken down the door and mated the bitch. Sixty three days later she had a litter of eight healthy pups, who are now having puppies of their own.

All bitches should be checked for infection by a vet before they are brought to the stud dog, but very few owners seem to consider that this is necessary. When a bitch is brought to be mated I also check that the bitch is ready, and the discharge is of the correct colour. But it is the owner's responsibility to bring the bitch on the right day.

After the mating we write all the particulars on a stud card and the stud fee is paid for one mating. It is up to the stud dog owner whether a second

Ruscombe Cassie with her first litter of six pups sired by Show Champion Beagold Louis.

mating is offered. We always offer a second mating, especially if the bitch is a maiden. It is always wise to keep all the information in writing such as the length of tie, the first day the bitch was noticed in season, and the date of mating – first and second time. If she misses because she was mated too early, then she can be mated at a later date, and vice versa. It is surprising how the memory plays tricks after six months, or whenever the bitch is next in season.

The bitch must also be in tip-top condition. They are usually in full coat and sparkling condition when they are in full season, that is nature's way of saying this is the time to produce puppies. We always worm our bitches when they come into season, if they are to be mated. After the mating she is returned to her kennel and lives a normal life, with extra food and vitamins being given after she is four weeks in whelp. The week before she is due to whelp we bring her into the whelping room so that she can get used to the surroundings, and scratch up the paper bedding into a nest, and make ready for the litter to arrive. The bitches who have had puppies before know immediately what is expected of them, and settle down to wait.

The first sign that the time is near, is when she pays a lot of attention to her rear end, licking herself and panting with the effort, numerous times throughout the day. She will need to relieve herself often. By this time she will be very round, and the signs that she is in whelp are unmistakable. We have found that most of our bitches over the years have whelped at night. This usually means that we sit up for three nights running. First watching and waiting to offer help if it is needed, then exhausted you leave your post, quite sure that nothing will happen and that is when she is sure to produce her first puppy.

If all is well, the others will follow at half hourly intervals. The troublesome ones have been at four hourly intervals. With bearded collies we have been needed as each puppy arrives, but with the border collies there have been no problems. We simply change the paper and watch the bitch cope on their own as each little creature comes into the world.

Whatever the breed, the mother likes to be left in peace to enjoy her pups on her own for the first week or two. It is always advisable to provide a whelping box for her out of the way of the usual comings and goings of the household. Even an outhouse that has heat, is preferable to a corner of a busy kitchen, where young children can interfere and intrude on the bitch's privacy.

Quite recently I heard of a collie bitch lying on four of her whelps and abandoning the rest of the litter. Children had been allowed to play with the pups even though they were only two weeks old. Then to cap it all, another bitch was allowed to come into the same room. In the wild state any bitch goes off on their own to have their pups, and then brings them up away from the rest of the pack, fighting viciously all the time for her privacy.

Many years ago I read a story about a border collie who had pups regularly, and each time the farmer put them down so that she could return to work the sheep, and not be debilated by feeding a litter. The bitch decided that she would have her pups away on her own, so whelped the litter in a stump of an old tree in the woods, creeping out at night to get food. The farmer tried to catch her and followed her whenever she was sighted so that he could find the litter and destroy it, but he was never successful. When the puppies were about six weeks old she led them down to the farm. The farmer and his wife were so overjoyed to see her again and her fat whelps that they did not have the heart to put them down. They were sold to local people in the village. The bitch never had another litter, but could be seen quite regularly visiting her children as they grew up. I believe there are hundreds of stories about the intelligent border collie but I will never forget this one.

CHAPTER THIRTEEN

Rearing

THERE was not a choice when we decided to run on Beagold Sugar Ray (Cassius-Bonnie) for show, as there were only two in the litter, a dog and bitch. The bitch was a nice black and white, beautifully made with an excellent temperament. She was sold to a show home, and we hope to meet her in the show ring later.

Sugar Ray's training started at four weeks, that means he was handled regularly, spoken to often, and encouraged to stand right from the beginning. He was a super fat puppy, good markings, and at that early stage it was clear that he would be a tri-colour, as small splodges of tan already showed between the black and white on his legs, and near his neck. He stood four square, with his tail down, his shape was excellent, and being so well constructed, he moved well.

The pups were weaned at five weeks, although Bonnie had plenty of milk and seemed to enjoy being with them. As she only had two, she was in beautiful condition throughout. The pups' diet consisted of boiled milk on Farleys rusks for breakfast. They loved the different taste and soon cleared the dish. After a couple of days they were given a dish of finely minced meat, served cooked. This they also cleaned up in double quick time. By now, they were looking out for the person who fed them and they also began to know when to expect their meals. We watched at every feed time to see that each pup was getting its fair share. It was soon apparent that the bitch was pushing the dog out and getting the lion's share, so they had their separate dishes at every meal. At first, we always give the food in one dish to encourage competition, a reluctant eater will see the other pups dash forward to eat and usually follows, taking mouthfuls before the food is cleared up. Once in the habit of dashing for food, they never seem to hang back.

By the time the pups were six weeks old they were on three meals a day. They were introduced to Gerber baby food, porridge, Farleys rusks, and different sorts of cereals. By giving them a wide variety, it accustoms them to different tastes before they go to their new homes. At lunch time they were given cooked minced meat with Oxo, or Bovril gravy on fine brown flour biscuit meal and the same was given again at evening meal.

Bonnie was still with them at night at this stage but at six weeks, she had had enough and returned to her kennel, leaving the puppies on their own in the whelping box and run. The puppies were already learning to be clean and always left their nest to go to the end of the run to defecate. Their nails were needle sharp and needed to be trimmed. Between six and eight weeks the puppies were wormed, and ten days later they were wormed again. Training continued every day. They were beautifully rounded healthy pups eating well, and sleeping through the night. There was always fresh water put down for them in a heavy stone drinking bowl.

The pups were now on four meals a day. For breakfast they had some sort of cereal, for their lunch we gave them a variety of high protein food mixed with biscuit meal. Sometimes it would be minced paunch, always cooked well or mincemeat, or fish. Twice a week they would have a part boiled egg added to the mixture. Vitamins such as Vetzymes, cod liver oil, and bone meal would also be added to their meal. Sometimes they would have Puppy Pedigree Chum, with mixer. Their dinner at 5pm was the same as lunch, and then at 10pm they were given the same as breakfast. With this mixed diet they thrived and gained weight considerably. The little bitch went to her new home and settled in well, with very little disturbance at night. Sugar Ray missed his partner and we had one or two noisy nights. But he soon settled down when he was made comfortable on a nice warm blanket in his kennel.

His training continued most days. A light leather collar was put on him while he played. He scratched it once or twice and then found too many other interesting things to amuse him. A lead was then attached to the collar, and he walked around the kitchen with the lead trailing. Then the lead was picked up and with just the slightest control, he was encouraged to follow. In no time, with plenty of encouragement, he followed willingly up and down the kitchen wherever he was led. With just a few minutes working every day, he was soon enjoying his training, especially as he was allowed to play as soon as he had responded to one or two commands.

The next step was to take him outside and with all the extra distractions this proved a little difficult. But he was encouraged to concentrate for a short time, to stand, move up and down on the lead, then stand again. The cars that flashed by worried him at first but as time progressed he learnt to ignore them, do his stint of training and then he was free to play.

However much training takes place at home, there is always the necessity to take the puppy to a place where other puppies are being trained for show. The distractions of cars are nothing compared to the natural wish to play with other dogs in the vicinity. Sugar Ray was taken regularly to a village hall and learnt to be handled by several trainers in the show handling classes.

This prepared him for his first visit to the show ring. When the big moment came he stood like a statue while the judge went over him and we were delighted. His movement was a little eratic, but that was to be expected as so many border collies weave from side to side when working. He glided along with his head in the correct position, on a loose lead and drew admiring remarks from those watching.

'Your dog looks as if he is working sheep here in the hall,' said one admiring on looker. What better compliment could we receive?

Sugar Ray had the full course of injections when he was twelve weeks old and fourteen weeks old. He had three meals a day until he was six months, then he went on to two meals a day and he ate up every scrap. He spent his days in the compound which is the size of a small field, chewing the apple trees, digging holes, destroying the hedge and barking at the birds. He was taken out in the car regularly so that he would get used to the long journeys travelling to shows. At first he was sick, but we gave him travel sickness pills and did not feed him before a journey and he soon got over the trouble. We also had the clever idea of bringing our very lively Bouvier bitch puppy on car trips with us. She did not give Sugar Ray a minute's peace, so he had no time to think about his nausea and soon he was travelling without any bother. In fact, he has now made his home in Finland and is proving to be a successful sire over there.

But while he was with us he was a happy dog, living as near as possible the life of freedom that his ancestors lived. I doubt whether every one of his ancestors worked sheep, but they lived in the country, had plenty of exercise, love and companionship and Sugar Ray lacked none of these.

Beagold Louis, his brother by a repeat mating was usually entered in the open dog class at championship shows so Sugar Ray was kept in the limit class. This was a regular arrangement and Sugar always took second place to his brother. But on one memorable day Sugar won the challenge certificate beating his brother, much to everyone's surprise.

Rearing a show puppy is slightly different to rearing a border that is to be kept simply as a pet. The show border collie has to be kept in super condition as long as possible, because show wins usually mean that the dog will be used at stud. The dog with a gleaming healthy coat, a well muscled body, a happy temperament, alert, lively and outgoing is the border collie that will do all the winning in the show ring. Its exercise and mode of living has to be good, even in to the veteran stage, if your choice is the show ring.

MENU:
If the bitch has a large litter, say over six, I supplement her feeding with a dish of Lactol milk for the pups, which they soon greedily lap up, once a day.

If there is one not putting on as much weight as the others I give it extra. Weaning the pups away from the mother usually starts at five weeks, when I feed finely minced beef to the pups early in the day with the Lactol milk and Farex in the evening.

At six weeks they will be on two milk meals and two meat meals. I add minced Pedigree Chum Mixer, or minced Purina to the meat and moisten with either Bovril or Marmite gravy. The bitch stays with the pups at night until they are seven weeks, and then she is taken away to her own kennel to grow her coat, build up her strength and have peace from her demanding family. By this time the pups are on four meals spread through the day. One milk meal in the early morning and three meat, supplement and biscuit meals throughout the day with the last feed is 10pm. Then they settle down happily for the night.

By eight weeks the pups are ready to go to their new homes. The variety of meals prepares them for the food they will receive over the next months, though I always give enough food for their first meal. I then recommend:

7.30am *Breakfast* Boiled cows milk, goats milk or powdered milk with some cereal, plus the correct amount of Stress. The yolk of an egg can be added to this meal three times a week. It can be varied with a meal of rice pudding or similar.

12.30pm *Lunch* Meat of some sort, tripe, rabbit, offal – minced or Pedigree Chum (Puppy) mixed with fine brown flour biscuit meal, plus minced or soaked Purina or Pedigree Chum Mixer added.

5pm as Lunch.

10pm as Lunch.

When the puppy is three months old, three meals can be given, spread throughout the day, then at twelve months old they only need two meals. These are obviously larger in quantity and I usually calculate one pound of meat plus the additives.

CHAPTER FOURTEEN

Show Winners

WE went to our first Border Collie of Great Britain Club Show in 1978 and that was the second that had been held. Bill Finlay was the judge and he had received an entry of one hundred and fifty eight borders, which was a very good entry for such a new club show. We were amazed to see so many borders at the venue, until we were told that the majority of the dogs and bitches were there for the obedience classes and in fact the number of entries for the whole show was six hundred and seventy six.

The exhibitors who entered their dogs for the beauty side of the show included Bob Henry with his dog Ellencliffe Brett who was entered in the puppy class and Mrs Ann Amos who won a first in the maiden class with Coires Sweep. Both Mr Henry and Mrs Amos have continued their interest in the breed both serving their turn as chairman of the Border Collie Club of Great Britain. Dusty and Mary Miller won open dog with Osoka Navajho of Firelynx, who is now a champion, and a veteran. Also entered in that class was Bruce and Sheena Kilsby's Gelert of Gawne from Whenway and Rhos of Rushmead CDX. Mrs Mary Gascoigne had travelled from Kent to exhibit her dog Kathmick Gary and Mrs Barbara Beaumont won minor puppy bitch with Bracken of Bluealloy. Barbara was later to become secretary of the Border Collie Club of Great Britain. Mrs Jean Hoare won the junior bitch class with Meg and Mrs Margaret Evans won special yearling with Una from Tracelyn. In the open bitch class Mr R. Somerscales won with Sweep of the Bothy, and second came Mrs Margaret Collier with Tevis Border Breeze.

We watched the judging with great interest, and met the organisers secretary Mrs Marion Leigh and treasurer Doug Collier. Most of the border collie owners that I have mentioned, have continued showing their dogs and also taken up judging the breed, so qualifying to give challenge certificates as specialist judges.

On reading through that catalogue we noticed that many of the dogs and bitches were born before the breed was recognised by the Kennel Club for show. It was not surprising that owners were keen to try another sport with this versatile breed. But what was surprising, was that so many of the exhibitors had entered their dogs in the beauty ring without first attempting a little basic training. The movement in many cases was erratic and impossible to assess. These same dogs were also entered in the obedience classes, and here it was obvious that hours had been spent training the dogs to make them near perfect on their sit and stays and heel work.

Many of the borders at the show were born from 1976 onwards. The veterans were Margaret Collier's Tevis Border Breeze whelped on January 4, 1971, Jean Hoare's Merrybrook Apache whelped on January 12, 1969, Mr Inskip's Jet whelped on August 8, 1971 and Miss Lilliman's Millwire Black Imp whelped on July 20, 1969. All these facts made fascinating reading, and seeing the dogs from before recognition, would help to build up a picture with future breeding in mind. The critique written by judge Bill Finlay pointed out one or two problems that should be watched for future breeding plans, especially as noticeable construction faults would be passed down from generation to generation.

The Border Collie Club of Great Britain held two shows in 1979. The first was in March, a limited to members show with Peter Newman, the all-round judge, officiating. We were delighted to win minor puppy and best puppy in show with Tilehouse Cassius at Beagold. Best in show was Mrs Mary Miller's Asoka Navajho of Firelynx.

The second show was a large open show with Mrs Ann Davis officiating. Her entry of two hundred and forty from one hundred and three dogs and bitches was excellent. The open obedience drew an entry of seven hundred and forty, which included many border collies, but other breeds as well. By that time there were more opportunities to enter open and championship shows. The societies realised that the border collie was being shown in large numbers so they gave us classes at championship shows without challenge certificates, and even then the classes were quite large. We always enjoyed showing our border collies so we entered as many shows as we could and were delighted to win several best of breed awards. The border was such an easy breed to take to shows, once bathed and groomed there was so little extra grooming needed to do on arrival at the show. Cassius won his first best of breed at the Scottish Kennel Club Championship Show in 1979 under the rough collie judge McLaren, who is famous for always wearing his kilt to shows. This was a very exciting win for us as Cassius was just ten months old. He continued winning well throughout the year, each time expertly handled by Felix Cosme and never came lower than second. Dog and handler caused quite a stir with their successful partnership in the show ring and there were many comments about Felix's professional approach to showing the border collie. He had gained an American Professional Handlers' Licence in

Contest of Champions.

America in 1973 when handling German shepherd dogs, so he was bringing a professionalism to the show ring that had never been seen among the border collie fraternity. There were also some adverse comments with some people saying that he was ruining the breed. Felix's answer was that he was showing the dog to emphasise its good points. The handler's job was to present his dog in the best possible light. By correcting the stance, placing the legs in line rather than letting the dog stand ten to two or cow hocked while the judge is looking, achieves the desired effect of presenting the dog to the judge in the best possible way. Some dogs although perfectly made in front and rear can stand wrongly when the judge is looking. Similar to a child slouching and putting all their weight on one foot, so distorting their body. Several other borders were doing well in the show ring. But we were particularly lucky at that time to be showing a young well made, good looking dog, who moved perfectly and answered most judges' interpretation of the breed standard. As 1979 drew to a close and we looked forward to similar successes in 1980.

In 1980 the Border Collie of Great Britain had H.A. Roberts officiating at their club show, again entries were good for both beauty and obedience. Our luck held out through 1980, and Cassius made history by winning so many best of breeds at championship shows that he gained the necessary points to be invited to compete at the prestigious contest of champions in 1981. It is a show held in London where the best dogs of all breeds who have gained the most points throughout the previous year compete in a match system for Top Dog of the Year. A panel of judges were to officiate at the Cunard International Hotel in London. A terrific amount of publicity is given to the contest and everyone is expected to wear evening clothes to the banquet. Pedigree Chum sponsor the contest and fabulous prizes are given to the lucky winners.

The day before the show, the Press tried to get all the competitors together to take photographs for the national papers. They were to be taken getting into a Daimler. But as none of the dogs enjoyed being in close contact with each other, the idea was doomed from the very beginning. At last after many unsuccessful attempts, the photographers made do with the toy, and standard poodle, kerry blue and glamorous lhasa apso getting into the car with their owners. Even then it was rather chaotic as the little lhaso tried to keep all the other dogs at bay. Cassius was left out of the picture as the Press and reporters thought a border collie did not fit into such glamorous company. Whether he was out of character or not, his behaviour was exemplary, even when he was admired and petted he took it all in his stride. It was a rare sight for a border collie and his owner to be seen walking through the palatial Cunard Hotel, for this was the dog that everyone visualised out in the country working sheep.

The contest started with each champion making a circuit around the ring. It wa a slippery floor with a red carpet across the middle of the circle, so when the dogs were sent around in a circle many were slipping and sliding on the part of the floor that was not covered. Of course, this affected the movement of the larger dogs, the tinies were not affected at all. The three judges who assessed Cassius had him moving up and down the carpet. There was a white join half way up the carpet and much to everyone's amusement, Cassius jumped over this divide without altering his stride. On his third journey up the carpet the audience were watching and applauding his graceful movement. He reached the final eight and had many opportunities to delight everyone with his super gliding movement.

In 1981 Cassius made history again by winning best of breed under Dutch judge Jo Kat. He then won through to reserve in the working group under judge Douglas Appleton at the Welsh Kennel Club championship show. He followed up with his marvellous first challenge certificate win at Crufts 1982, making history again by being the first border collie to win this award. The judge was Mrs Catherine Sutton. Six months later, Cassius won the title of show champion at the National Working Breeds championship show under

Show Champion Muirend Border Dream.

judge Bill Finlay. The same day Mrs Nan Simpson's bitch Muirend Border Dream was the first bitch to win her title of show champion. In all Border Dream won five challenge certificates and was then taken out of the show ring for her maternal duties.

Another dog who won well in 1982 was Dusty and Mary Miller's Asoka Navajho of Firelynx. He was winning best of breeds in 1978, so it was not surprising that during that first year he gained his title winning his first challenge certificate under judge Bill Dixon at Birmingham championship show in May, his second was under judge David Samuels at Leeds in July and his third challenge certificate and title were awarded at the Welsh Kennel Club championship show under judge Mrs Prue Green in August. This was the record for a border gaining his title in the shortest time. Muirend Border Dream gained the record for being made up to show champion in the shortest time for bitches. Another first for Navajho came when he won the veteran class at the first championship show held by the Border Collie Club of Great Britain.

Bruce and Sheena Kilsby's Tork of Whenway won his first challenge certificate at the Working Breeds of Scotland championship show in 1982 under judge Mrs Marion Leigh. Then he won two of his challenge

Ian and Vicky Mitchell's Show Champion Welsh Queen Bess.

certificates at Crufts 1983 and 1984. Ian and Vicky Mitchell's Welsh Queen Bess also won her first challenge certificate in 1982, but it was not until 1984 that she gained her title.

Eric Broadhurst's Show Champion Tracelyn Gal gained her title in the first three years. Mrs Gina Croft's Show Champion Melodor Flurry at Falconmoor was best of breed at Crufts and then went on to be the first bitch to win reserve in the working group at Crufts under judge Joe Braddon. Mrs Hazel Monk's Show Champion Whenway Juanity of Monkfield was sired by Show Champion Asoka Navjho of Firelynx out of Whisp of Whenway. She was the first show champion to be made up that was sired by a show champion. Mrs Mary Gascoigne's Show Champion Kathmick Griff and John Ritchie's Show Champion Melodor Flint of Dykebar were also made up to show champions in 1984. Mrs Di Lewin's Show Champion Mizanne the Witch was the first prick eared bitch made up and she gained her title in 1985. Bob Henry's Black Shadow of Ettaswell, Tony and Karen Holliday's Whenway Hope of Corinlea, and Eric Broadhurst's Rosehurst Twilight Crystal gained their titles in 1985. There are still several dogs and bitches that have one or two challenge certificates but have not yet been lucky enough to gain their titles by winning that illusive third.

*Ian and Vicky Mitchell's
Bonnie Prince Charlie.*

*Show Champion Melodor
Flint of Dykebar.*

Line-up of winners at the North-West Border Collie Club open show. Show Champion Beagold Louis (centre) was best in show.

In 1986 Mrs Chris Mclean's Melodor Robbie gained his title, he was sired by Muirend Border Reiver out of Muirend Border Ballard of Melodor, true Scottish breeding. Our Show Champion Beagold Louis was the youngest dog to gain his title at the present time. He was only twenty nine months on the day of the show – May 25 1986. He won it at the Bath championship show under judge Ken Bullock. Ross and Vicky Green's Show Champion Tilehouse Tipp gained his title at the Southern Counties championship show when I judged on May 30, 1986. Kathy Lister made up her bitch now Show Champion Fieldbank Merrymeg by winning the third challenge certificate at Crufts 1986 under judge Mrs Ann Davis.

There are several reserve challenge certificate winners waiting to gain full recognition. As they are younger dogs and bitches, one or two have show champion parents. There are also several quality dogs and bitches that have not yet been lucky enough to win the reserve challenge certificate although they are shown regularly, and win quite often at open shows where the breed is now quite often classified. Sometimes it can be put down to an unpopular colour, or slight mismarking. A beautifully made handsome dog or bitch can

*Ross Green's Show
Champion Tilehouse Tipp.*

*Show Champion
Snowmere Tweed.*

Jan Goddard's border collies. Show Champion Huntroyde Beau Brummel is pictured right.

be held back when the final choice is being made because of light tri-colouring, or what may be termed a light eye, or uneven markings, or unusual colouring. Miss Julie Mockford's Show Champion Snowmere Tweed, sired by Gemond Castor out of Megan of Snowmere is a very handsome, well made tri-coloured dog, but the mixture of the sable colour in his coat can either please the judge, or put the judge off placing him. That is regardless of his excellent movement and the fact that he is trained for show with perfection.

Brian and Jan Goddard's Show Champion Huntroyde Beau Brummel at Sanrian won his first challenge certificate at Crufts and has won constantly at open shows, even going to best in show and reserve best in show all breeds. Unfortunately, he was held back winning his title at the crucial time in his life when he became ill and lost coat and condition for a time. He has regained his health now after loving and careful treatment and will continue to take his place with the winners.

Ross and Vicky Green's Show Champion Tilehouse Tipp is a dog that can look outstanding in any company. But he can also look dejected and uninterested in the whole proceedings. This has held him back from winning his title earlier. Kathy Lister's Show Champion Fieldbank Professional is now a veteran but has only just gained his title. His construction is excellent and he behaves perfectly in the show ring. I personally believe that he has been held back because of his colouring, his light grey with the tri-colour is slightly unusual.

The bitches have a more difficult time to get made up to show champions, so many are taken out of the show ring to have puppies and then it takes time for them to return to their show condition. In fact, there are quite a few excellent quality bitches just waiting for their lucky break. Mrs Jean Hoare's Merrybrook Apache made the transition from working sheep and a successful obedience career to the show ring, proving to all the doubters that it can be done. She won her way to the top in 1979 with twenty best of breed wins, then at twelve and a half years of age she won the Pedigree Chum Stakes class for best veteran at the Border Union championship show. Meg of Merrybrook was one of the reserve challenge certificate winners at Leeds in 1982. David and Jean Hoare's latest show champion is Merrybrook Lisa. They are the first breeders to export a bitch – Merrybrook Sophia – to New Zealand. They then brought her back in whelp to New Zealand champion Aberdeen Boy of Clan Abby. Her puppies were born in quarantine and are

Show regulars:
Angela Gillespie
Ray Simpson
Tony Holliday.

Show Champion Viber travelling Matt from Corinlea, set a new record with 11 challenge certificates in 1988.

now in the show ring and of these they kept Merrybrook Laura and Merrybrook Josh.

Karen and Tony Holliday show regularly at championship shows, their winning dog Firelynx Chiri Gvano of Corinlea was a multiple first prize winning at open and championship shows with several best of breeds to his credit. Another of their well known winners was Show Champion Whenway Hope of Corinlea, a handsome black and white rough coated dog that has now won his title. Their latest winning dog is also a junior warrant winner, Show Champion Viber Travelling Matt from Corinlea winner of ten challenge certificates so far.

Their most recent bitches to gain their titles are Show Champion Corinlea Rona, a home bred bitch, and Show Champion Ruscombe Astra at Corinlea, and there are others just waiting to win their titles in the near future.

When we first visited the Scottish shows we saw some excellent quality border collies on their home ground. Well known and winning dogs are exhibited regularly by Mrs Chris McLean and her Show Champion Melodor Robbie has done a lot of winning. Mrs Janet Hastie has a very successful winner in her Show Champion Lethans Hopeful Flame, winner of the challenge certificate at Crufts in 1987 and 1988. He is sired by Kirkfield Kirk out of Kirkfield Shell. He is the litter brother to Cluff of

Mobella Midnight Cowboy (Tally Of Mobella-Falconmoor Highland Fling at Mobella). Pictured with Mrs Pam Harris.

Cluff Of Mobella (Kirkfield Kirk ex Kirkfield Shell).

Karen Holliday presents Muirend Border Gypsy for the judge's inspection.

Mobella owned by Mrs Pam Harris. It was also in Scotland that we met the winning dogs and bitches from Mrs Nan Simpson's Muirend breeding. When she travels down to England it is a sure thing that she will take back the challenge certificate and best of breed. John Ritchie has skillfully piloted his Show Champion Melodor Flint of Dykebar to great heights, he is a well known quality dog who has so far won eight challenge certificates.

It can be noticed from this string of show champions that black and white, rough coated border collies feature strongly in the popularity stakes, followed by tri-coloured. Blue merle and red merle seldom feature in the winning line up, and as yet none have won top honours. Red and white borders are beginning to be very popular and we were delighted to win with our Show Champion Passims Bonnie at Beagold. She certainly stands out with her very dark colouring and classic white markings and is the first red/white show champion. Mrs Hazel Monk is also doing well with her red and white Tracelyn Dolly Bird of Melodor, winning a reserve challenge certificate in 1986 and the reserve challenge certificate at Crufts 1988.

Tipped ears or active ear carriage are what most judges look for, pricked ears only seldom are at the head of the winning line-up, even when all the other essentials are there in the dog or bitch. There are only two pricked eared bitches that win regularly – Show Champion Mizanne the Witch and her daughter Show Champion Mizanne the Lady Lucinda. Smooth coated border collies receive very little consideration in the show ring. The breed clubs sometimes classify classes for the smooth coated border collie but the entry is only made from one or two.

Specialist judges do not tend to penalise light brown eyes to any degree, but it is more noticeable that all round judges look for the darker eye as required by so many other breeds. The light eyes does show up as giving a hard expression in the black and white border.

Mrs Angela Gillespie is rarely seen at open or championship shows with less than seven or eight well behaved border collies. Her Detania prefix is very well known and I have heard many open show secretaries praise Angela for saving the day and boosting an entry that otherwise would be low. But now the breed is so well established that we have lost the tag of being poor relation to the rough collie and at some championship shows our border collie entries far exceed all the other collie breeds.

CHAPTER FIFTEEN

Border Collie Clubs

THERE are three border collie clubs at the moment and the Scottish Border Collie Club and the East Anglian Border Collie Club are in the process of being formed. The first was the Border Collie Club of Great Britain, established in 1976. The next to be formed was the Southern Border Collie Club in 1979 and the North West Border Collie Club was established in 1984. Each club caters for the border collie in areas all over Great Britain.

It is amazing to see the great interest that has arisen in showing the breed, even at shows where obedience is not classified. The first club shows had to put on obedience classes to draw the entries. The exhibitors entered for the obedience and then decided that while they were at the show, they would have a go in the breed ring. The Border Collie Club of Great Britain has several branches and they held their first championship show on March 16, 1985. Best in show was John Ritchie's Show Champion Melodor Flint at Dykebar. It was a well run show, and a milestone in the history of the breed. Tom Horner was the judge and drew an entry of over five hundred. Of course, this was an impossible task for one judge to perform and so Bill Dixon was called in. This club holds one open show and one championship show each year at the Newark and Nottinghamshire Showground. The large venue is needed as there is always a huge entry.

The Southern Border Collie Club's first championship show was held in April 1986, a most enjoyable show, beautifully decorated with flags and flowers and the committee gave a warm welcome to the exhibitors. Our dog Show Champion Tilehouse Cassius at Beagold won best in show. The North West Border Collie Club always has a friendly atmosphere at its shows. They also have enough confidence to plan their shows with two judges for the twenty nine classes. Four of the classes at their open show are: special open dog (smooth coated), special open dog (any colour except black and white and tri-colour) and the same two classes for the bitches. This attracts extra entries from people who have very little chance winning with the variety of colours and it gives the not so popular smooth coated border collies a chance to win. If these specials are put on regularly I can see exhibitors keeping their smooth coated and unusual coloured dogs, knowing that they have a chance to compete against each other, rather than always coming up against the more popular types.

Names and Addresses

The Border Collie Club of Great Britain,
Acting Secretary: Mrs Joy Russell, 15 Chapel Lane, Cosby,
Leicestershire.
   Tel: 0533 864 850.

The Southern Border Collie Club.
Secretary Miss Monica Boggia, Broomhirst, Willow Wood, Whitstable, Kent.
   Tel: 0227 274324.

North West Border Collie Club
Secretary: Mrs Richardson, 61 Rosegarth Avenue, Aston, Sheffield.

Two more Clubs are in the process of being recognised by the Kennel Club:
The Scottish Border Collie Club, acting Secretary Mrs Chris McLean.

The East Anglian Border Collie Club, acting Secretary Mrs Jenifer Garner, 177 Holme Court Avenue, Biggleswade, Bedfordshire.

With five Border Collie Clubs in such a widespread area of Great Britain the show border collie is well catered for, especially as most of the clubs hold regular training sessions, for show and obedience. The Border Collie Club of Great Britain also has branches in several different areas.

CHAPTER SIXTEEN

The Border Collie Abroad

Australia and New Zealand

THE first border collies were imported to Australia in the middle of the nineteenth century. They consequently found their way to New Zealand and have formed the basis of the breed.

The first borders were shown at the Sydney Royal in 1933 in the variety classes and the breed was registered in the Canine Stud Book of Australia in 1945. In October 1950 the Kennel Control of Victoria said the breed would be allowed to be shown at championship shows as from January 1 1951 and since that early date, top quality border collies have been bred by several kennels, many used for work, but also with such excellent quality that many won well in the beauty show competitions. They were originally shown in the non-sporting group, then in 1953 a separate group was formed and the border collie was in the ring with the Australian cattle dog and the Australian kelpie, but it was not until 1963 the Australian National Kennel Control adopted the first national standard.

The breeders have had so many more years to establish a show type without losing the instinct to work. Although they now accept the red and white colouring, it is quite obvious that black and white, profuse coats, and perfectly even markings are one of their main criteria when breeding the show border collie. Whether we in Great Britain admire this advancement or not, other countries quite often go to Australia for their foundation stock. They have formed the opinion that our border collies would look out of place in their show rings as our dogs do not have the length of coat that they favour. We allow in our standard, pricked, tipped and uneven ears, and our dogs are much higher on leg. From pictures that I have studied of the Australian dogs, I would say that they have heavier bone and carry much more weight than ours do. But in all, I would say that they have not been altered so drastically as a breed. True, they have set a type and bred closely for that type, but they still claim that their dogs would work if called upon to do so.

As far as I know there has only been one import of a border collie show bitch and that was Mrs Jean Hoare's Merrybrook Sophie after she had been mated to New Zealand champion Aberdeen of Clan-Abby. The litter was born in quarantine in August 1986 and the puppies were sold to keen show exhibitors. New Zealand has about twenty border collie breeding kennels and is well established in the show ring and being such a versatile breed is also worked. The showgoers are also in the happy position of being able to make their dogs up to Australian/New Zealand champions, as other breeds can win the dual title on the Continent and in the United States and Canada.

UNITED STATES OF AMERICA

The border collie is not recognised as a breed in the States. Border collie owners still believe that the border collie should only be a working dog and if the American Kennel Club recognised the breed for show, they consider that breeders would start breeding for appearance only. We have found that even four generations away from the working ancestors, there are often two or three in each litter that are typical workers with very strong working instincts. As I have mentioned before, border collies bred on farms from working parents do not necessarily have the gift to work. In fact, that is how so many are either sold or put down because the farmers recognise the lack of working instinct in certain puppies.

We have proved that there is wide open space in the show ring for this versatile breed, without stepping on the toes of the obedience workers or the working dogs. What has progressed here in Great Britain could well take place in the States and the border collie could eventually be recognised for show in the working group.

We have exported a number of our dogs to the States. The breed is allowed to be shown in American Kennel Club shows in the miscellaneous classes and a Breed Standard has been drawn up.

HEAD: Essentially old fashioned collie type head – fairly broad skull, slightly blunt in muzzle.

STOP: Very moderate.

BITE: Scissor.

TEETH: Of good size.

EARS: Medium broad at base and tapering towards tip. Carried prick or semi-erect, or variation of either.

EYES: Fairly large, can be dark, light or blue, or combination of either, but dark are favoured. Expression, bold in action, soft and appealing at rest.

BODY: Slightly longer than high. Back line straight from withers to loin, with slight rise over loin. Chest adequate for build of dog. Forelegs straight, forearm muscular, feet oval, high-arched with thick heavy pads. Hind legs long and wide set, with hocks well let down.

FEET: Oval high arched with pads heavy enough for tough field work.
TAIL: Set on low and carried low with slight upward swirl.
COAT: Very dense of varied lengths, can be rough, medium, or smooth. Rough or medium coats may be wavy or slightly curly – forelegs and hindlegs on rough and medium dogs well feathered with mane slightly to well abundant.
COLOURS: Black, grey, blue merle, white or chocolate with white points, such as collar, chest, feet, tip of tail and on face and body, however majority will be black with white markings.
SIZE: Height dogs average 18" to 24" at shoulder. Bitches 17" to 22". It is not uncommon for dogs and bitches to be of the same size.
WEIGHT: 30 to 60 lbs. (American International Border Collie Registry).

By publishing a standard as a guideline for breeders, it is just a very short step for exhibitors to become dedicated showgoers, as we are in Great Britain.

SCANDINAVIA

Norway and Sweden have recently recognised the breed and in Finland Mrs Raija-Wahlman Leinonen bought a challenge certificate winning tri-colour dog, Beagold Sugar Ray from us. They intend to use him to start their own line of tri-colour border collies. Breeders in Finland have also imported a breeding pair from New Zealand.

SPAIN

In the Spanish dog magazine 'Los Perros', the editor Angel-Antonio Torres Rio has included a very interesting article on the border collie and he says: 'We await to see the border collie very soon in Spain, as well as the rest of the Continent for work as well as the show ring'.

They feature many very good photographs of British show border collies, including Chris McLean's Show Champion Melodor Flurry at Falconmoor winning reserve in the working group at Crufts 1984. In 1974 Mr Angell-Antonio Torres Rio imported various border collies into Spain, but as they had not been recognised by the English Kennel Club and were unregistered, he could not register them or show them. In 1980 Mr Francisco Soro Gonsalvez introduced the registered border collie and showed them in the beauty ring. He imported a breeding pair, so the first litter of registered border collies in Spain were born in 1982. His first champion was Kirkfield Kaley. He was made up in 1983 to a World Champion when he won at the World Championship show in Madrid 1983. His second champion was Champion Don Carlo of Tracelyn, both being English bred dogs.

HOLLAND

The well known collie kennel that excelled in borders in Holland was Joe and Betty Kat's Maramin Kennels, advertised as the home of champion rough and smooth collies, shelties and border collies. Maramin Betty is the world's first border collie champion under FCI regulations. She has also obtained the required number of tickets to qualify her for her International Champion's title in Holland. Mr and Mrs Kat were the only border collie exhibitors to advertise their show dogs in the English Dog World Magazine. Sadly Mr Joe Kat died two years ago, but was able to judge border collies at the Amsterdam Winners Show 1986, just before he died.

CHAPTER SEVENTEEN

Buying the Border Collie as a Pet

WE frequently receive requests for a puppy to go solely as a house pet and companion. Before going any further, we give the potential owner a detailed talk about the border collie's character and the requirements of the adult dog or bitch. If there is any chance that the puppy is to live in a flat, or in the middle of a large town where it will not receive adequate exercise, we try to persuade the buyer to consider a less active breed, a smaller quieter type of dog that needs less attention and exercise.

The border collie, like the bearded collie needs an outdoor active kind of owner, that will dedicate himself to training the dog to keep its brain alert and its body continually on the move. The border collie needs regular daily exercise and lots of freedom. It is no use thinking it will be satisfied in a small garden with a four foot fence to keep it in. In next to no time, the dog will leap the fence and be away. People often argue that they know all about the breed because they or their parents owned one many years ago. From further discussion, it becomes apparent that the animal they had was a cross breed, that looked like a border collie because it was black and white. They were given no papers when they purchased the dog and it could well have come from a pet home, or a puppy farm.

There are some reputable pet shops, many of them well known, where considerable care is taken with the stock offered for sale. Unfortunately, there are quite a few others where cross bred puppies are sold and given names of the breed they resemble. The stock is bought in as a marketable commodity and the health and welfare of the dog is of secondary importance. Yet by the nature of the trade, the risk of infection is great. Puppies of all breeds bought in from different places can pass disease to each other quicker than lightning. After purchase, the puppy might be sick on the journey home. The jolting of the car might be blamed but the poor creature could already be affected with some illness. Then a massive vet's bill is incurred in order to cure the puppy – all because of an unwise purchase.

I receive many enquiries for puppies and when the potential purchaser hears the price, they prefer to phone around for the cheapest pup on offer.

But the cheapest is not usually the healthiest. If you go to a reputable breeder and something is wrong with your pup, the breeder is only too keen to help put the matter right, they have their reputation to guard. They have planned the litter, fed it correctly, wormed and weaned it, and prepared it for its new home so consequently all risks are at a minimum.

Many years ago a puppy was bought from a pet show with papers naming the breed as a border collie. At six months the puppy was taken to training school and immediately the owner was told that it was not a pure bred border collie. Even if the pup had been pure bred, they had paid an exorbitant price, and so the disappointed owners ended up with nothing but a very expensive cross bred dog. The colour was right, the markings were good enough, but there was definitely foreign blood running through the veins of the poor little no-name pup. By the time they returned to the pet shop to complain and hopefully to be reimbursed, the shop had changed hands, and the new owners had no knowledge of the previous owners' whereabouts.

We are always delighted to find homes for our puppies where the owners are active, youngish and keen to dedicate themselves and their dogs to some training programme. The best owners are those who regularly go on long walks, the families who spend their weekends in the open air, actively involved in mountain climbing or some other leisure pursuit. The dogs love it, and the owner could not have a better breed to share such an active life. With enough exercise the border collie will become a marvelous companion, intelligent, easy to groom and an excellent guard if ever called upon to do so.

As already mentioned there are a number of border collie clubs, as well as obedience clubs in most towns, and now agility clubs, where the clever border collie is made more than welcome.

The border collie is no more difficult to control than many other breeds when they have been brought by unsuitable owners. I always marvel at the foolishness of elderly ladies buying great danes, Rottweillers, or St. Bernards as house pets. Then there are the large families that live in small crowded houses and include large dogs in their homes. Problems usually arise and then the poor dog turned out, left to roam at will or at best put on the rescue scheme.

We give a menu and a list of instructions to all the new owners and ask them to telephone us at any time for help or advice to resolve any problems with the puppy that might arise. We ask them to phone before the problem becomes a habit which would be much more difficult to correct. We describe the liveliness of the dogs, and the quieter but sharper character of the bitches. We also remind the new owner that the bitch will come into season usually twice a year and must be kept carefully shut up. If the new puppy is to be just a pet, the only decision left to make is the colour and sex. The standard points can be of little interest, unless there is the slightest chance that they might decide to show. Then of course we have to go into the requirements needed for the show border collie.

Too many new owners collect their eight week old puppy and take it into their home without any preparations and no idea of what is entailed in owning a pup of any breed. They soon realise that it is not just a cuddly toy, and find that it will not sit quietly while it is admired and spoilt. The pup could well be quiet and shy at first, taking time to get used to its new surroundings, feeling rather overpowered by the different noises and smells, and a little sad as it could be missing its littermates. The first puddle on the carpet will be accepted and cleaned up, even the first mess might be laughed off. It is when the messes become larger and the puddles more regular and distributed over a much wider area that the rose coloured spectacles disappear. The irate owner then starts to get strict and the puppy is banished to a corner of the kitchen or even put outside in a shed. From being petted and spoilt at the outset, the poor pup is confused, unsettled and very unhappy. It is not surprising that it is not sure where it can mess or wet. We try to explain all this before the puppy leaves our kennels. We try to instil the information and suggestions concerning the comfort, training and welfare, glossing over none of the drawbacks, and even emphasing the difficulties that will be experienced before the puppy becomes clean and uses the correct place at the right time.

A place should be set aside for the puppy to call his own. When he is shut in, any mess will therefore be confined to a small area. A sleeping box or benched bed, large enough for the pup to stretch out on, should be provided with another small area covered with sheets of newspaper and torn up paper to soak up water. A barricade, high enough to contain the puppy at night or when left alone during the day is useful. It also helps if you leave a bone or toy for the pup to play with, plus fresh water and a couple of biscuits. The puppy should be put outside last thing at night and first thing in the morning until he gets the idea that the garden is the place to do his jobs. If there is a cosy outside shed or outhouse where a day bed can be arranged, that will teach him to play and enjoy himself outside, with freedom to choose when he will rest and when he will play. With sensible but firm training the pup will soon learn what is expected of him. Before long he can be taken into other rooms in the house that he will respect and everyone will be surprised and pleased that the pup will bark to be let out.

The next lesson will be to teach the pup to walk without pulling on the lead and behave when he is taken out in the car. Never allow the puppy to bark or jump about. It might be amusing when the pup is small, but later on this riotous behaviour can be both annoying and dangerous. Stop any bad behaviour right at the very beginning or it will become a habit and impossible to break. Puppies bought as pets usually come into a family where there are children. No child should be allowed to tease or play to boisterously with a young pup. So many times I receive calls from annoyed parents who tell me the puppy is biting the children. It always turns out that the puppy is retaliating from being constantly pulled about and teased. I would never knowingly sell a puppy to a family where there are several young children who will treat the puppy like another toy.

Sometimes it is the adults who complain that the puppy is biting their fingers. Of course, they should never give the puppy the opportunity to bite them. I always tell new owners never to allow the puppy to bite, even when it is very young. Always play with something like a rubber ring or a rubber bone. The puppy will pull and chew the toy you are playing with and never get into the habit of biting. The border collie puppy sometimes chases his owner in the garden when he is playing and bites at their heels of the shoes. A quick turn around and smack stops this natural inclination to move you along. When the puppy is playing with its littermates, it needs a certain time for rest and it will disappear into a corner or go off on its own to sleep. If it is never allowed peace, it will bite when disturbed and who can blame it?

CHAPTER EIGHTEEN

General Care

The border collie is a very healthy animal if it is kept in the right conditions with plenty of exercise, love, companionship and an interest in life such as obedience or agility training. The basic training needed for the show ring, plus the outings to shows also keeps the dog's mind active and interested. We will never sell our puppies to people who just want the border collie as a house pet or a playmate for their children. It is not the breed to be happy and satisfied living such a sedentary life.

Puppies should be taken to have their hard pad, distemper, leptospirosis and parvo virus jabs when they are about twelve weeks and fourteen weeks, or the age suggested by the vet. Then, they only need regular booster injections. The border collie is such a healthy dog that it is only when accidents occur or if some unusual symptoms develop, that a visit to the vet is needed. Even the bitch in whelp takes very little notice of her condition and any owner trying to curb the bitch's wish for exercise as her time to whelp draws near, will find it practically impossible. They are sensible enough to know their own capabilities, so it is best to give them credit for intelligence. They will not damage the litter by over activity. We have bred several litters and each time the bitch has coped perfectly with the birth, then settled down to suckle her young with no extra help. They are just perfect mothers. Perhaps we have been lucky, but I have not heard of any problems at the birth of border collie puppies. We provide heat for the puppies in their whelping box and we make sure the mother has all the care and comfort that we give to other breeds. She might not need it, but she certainly does appreciate it. We also ensure that every puppy in the litter is given the same attention, regardless of colour or mismarking. There is no question of the survival of the fittest or the best in our breeding programme.

Because many show owners look after their borders very conscientiously, grooming them every week, feeding them well and regularly and housing them comfortably, it does not mean that they are trying to alter the breed in any way. A well groomed dog is a happy dog. It is a beautiful sight and one to be proud of. A well fed dog of any breed can sparkle with health and fight off illness which keeps the vet's bills to a minimum. Whether the dog is kept in the house or kennelled outside, it should have a place to stretch out or a bed to curl up in. There should not be any draughts or dampness and the area should be well ventillated for the warmer days of summer, with adequate shelter from the rain. The dogs love to have freedom outside but they do need to have a haven of their own. This, I believe is a small return for the love and companionship that they give to their owners.

Most of us have bought our border collies from farms at one time and have seen the way many are kept. I remember seeing a nice little bitch chained to a small kennel that was just large enough for her to curl up in and the chain was just long enough for her to defecate outside the kennel. There was corrugated sheet on top of the kennel to keep out the rain and that was all the comfort the bitch had. Another time, we saw a litter of pups running in a huge earth floored barn that had rat holes and vermin tunnels leading outside. That certainly was a case of survival of the fittest. I also recall seeing a dog living in a hole in the wall of a barn lying on filthy straw. These dogs were called upon to work but they were given no repayment for their efforts.

FEEDING

I have already mentioned the menu we give to our puppies from weaning time to the day they go to their new homes. We provide the new owner with a dish of food and a list of food that the pup is used to eating. That means the puppy does not have an upset tummy coping with a different diet as well as a new environment. We suggest that the new owner continues with four meals a day until the puppy is twelve weeks old, then one of the milk meals can be left out. The three meals for the twelve week old puppy are breakfast which consists of cereal with boiled milk and with added vitamins. Lunch at 1pm and dinner at 7pm can be meat and biscuit. This can be a complete feed, Pedigree Chum, tripe, ox cheek, or heart. A wide range of different feeds can be given, so long as the dog is used to a variety.

As the dog gets older and it is clearly thriving – nicely covered with flesh but not too fat – it will only need two meals a day. This is usually by the time the dog is about eighteen months old. Some dogs like to have the same food day after day. If they keep healthy on their diet and enjoy their meal, there is no need to alter it. Extras can be given, such as mixing the meat and biscuit with gravy made from oxo or bovril. Vetzyme tablets and Stress can be given even when the dog becomes adult. If the coat looks dull and lifeless it is a good tip to add a teaspoon of vegetable oil to the dinner. Most dogs love to chew marrow bones, it keeps their teeth clean and keeps them amused for hours.

HEALTH

It is advisable for owners to have their border collies tested for hip dysplasia, then if the owner puts the papers through the KC/BVA scheme they can claim in advertisements that the dogs have been certified as 'Examined radiographically and certified under the KC/BVA Scheme'. In fact, all dogs should be checked for hip dysplasia before they are bred from or used at stud.

We also have our dogs checked for eye problems. Progressive retinal atrophy and collie eye anomaly could become a problem in the breed if affected dogs and bitches were used for breeding. A list of those with certificate 'Clear' is published in many of the club magazines.

Hip dysplasia can be hereditary, but other suggestions have been put forward such as over exercising at a young age or over feeding so that the heavy body can cause lameness when the puppy is allowed to over exercise. The result of this disorder can result in a dog being crippled.

Progressive retinal atrophy is hereditary. A temporary certificate can be given to dogs tested when they are two years old. A permanent certificate will be given if the dog is tested again after three years of age. Permanent blindness will affect the dog eventually.

Collie eye anomaly can be hereditary. It is advisable that those affected are never used at stud and bitches affected should not be bred from. Affected dogs will not go blind, but could have tunnel vision.

The best time to check you dog is when you are grooming. Any problems are then noticed before they get established. Ears should be clean, eyes dry and bright, with no discharge. Teeth can be cleaned either with a tooth scraper or brushed clean. Nails will keep short if the dog is allowed to run on a hard surface, but if only exercised on grass they will need to be cut. Check that the dew claws are not too long. Regular grooming keeps the dog healthy. The border collie drops coat usually in the summer, great tufts fall out at the first moulting, until your handsome well coated dog looks high on leg and very unkempt. A good bath will remove surplus coat, and allow the new coat to grow quickly.

Ailments

Border collies are very healthy animals, unlike many other breeds they are not prone to disorders of many kinds. We have had slight stomach upsets from over eating, but our only regular visits to the veterinary surgeon are for the usual injections and the collection of worm tablets. We have all our dogs and bitches tested for hip dysplasia, progressive retinal atrophy and collie eye anomaly. From then on, we have been very lucky and had no problems that we could not attend to ourselves. We had a dog who got a sore throat from excess barking and another who got splinters in the throat from chewing the woodwork but a dose of cough syrup soon put the matter right.

STOMACH UPSET AND DIARRHOEA
Feeding a good quality, mixed diet will help the dog to keep in good condition. But sometimes the motion is loose and it could follow that the dog has eaten a more than substantial meal of raw meat or uncooked paunch. Sometimes the paunch, or tripe is very dark in colour and that could well affect the faeces. But diarrhoea tinged with blood is very serious and a vet should be called without delay. It could be that the dog has eaten chicken or rabbit bones that could cause the blood, but if he has not, some other cause may be diagnosed. For an ordinary stomach upset we give a dose of milk of magnesia, especially if the dog vomits a watery yellow mess. Some dogs might suffer from constipation, they can be seen to strain and pass nothing, a desert spoonful of olive oil or liquid paraffin will give relief.

DANDRUFF
Dogs with black coats sometimes suffer from scurfy conditions. A regular weekly shampoo with one of the advertised human shampoos will soon rectify the problem. Add a little suet, or margarine to the diet.

ECZEMA
The first sign is a patch of wet hair on the legs or part of the body. The dog will lick it constantly until the sore place is red and raw. Clean the wound with TCP, but it is important to have the vet attend to the trouble.

HERNIA
It is unusual in our breed for a puppy to be born with a small umbilical hernia. In affected dogs the hernia often disappears as the puppy grows older. But if it becomes larger or if the hernia is in the groin, the vet should be consulted and will decide if an operation is necessary.

HYSTERIA
The border collie is a very active dog and is sometimes too active. Wild uncontrolled behaviour from a very young puppy can develop into fits of hysteria. We always advocate that a puppy is never allowed to get over excited. There may be one in the litter who never rests and keeps the rest on the go all the time. When a puppy goes to its new home it should be made to rest regularly. There should be a short time for play and a longer time to rest. Hysteria could be caused by eating too fast, then rushing around. The

pup could also be badly infected with worms or suffering from indigestion. With one occurance of hysteria a dose of milk of magnesia will settle the puppy, but if the attack continues the vet should be consulted.

STINGS
The inquisitive border could well be stung by a bee or wasp. The sting must be taken out and then the affected area should be rubbed with TCP or vinegar. If the swelling remains, the vet should be called to give an anti-histamine injection.

TEETH
I am sure no other breed constantly chew and damage their teeth like the border. Nothing is safe. They can jump up over six feet high and little by little, devour a cross beam in the kennel. The only unappetising unchewable wall is a steel or iron one. The dogs have huge exercise areas and it is not the door to freedom that is damaged. It is the side of the wall or the roof of the sleeping compartment. A chair or sleeping bench is devoured so completely that it disappears into lumps of unidentified objects. It is not because they are bored. The dogs return from a long walk and instead of resting like any other breed, they are looking around for mischief. I have retrieved splinters from their gums, cleaned their teeth from the silver marks left after they have chewed their feeding bowls, and washed their mouths from licking paint work. It is surprising to find that some of them do collect tartar even with all this activity. We scrape the tartar away then clean their teeth with a brush.

WORMS
We dose our puppies with tablets from the vet at five weeks then again at seven weeks just before they go to their new homes. We have only had roundworms to contend with. But we advise the new owner to check that all is well and that the puppy does not lose condition, which could be attributed to the first worming not being successful. Another dose of worm tablets or liquid should be given at about four months of age, just to make sure that the pup is completely clear.

If the puppy has the signs of tapeworms – constant scavenging plus general loss of condition – then it is more difficult to eradicate. Special treatment from the vet is needed.

FLEAS, LICE AND TICKS
Every effort should be made to keep your border free of these external parasites. During the summer months it is easy for them to pick up fleas from a country walk or off a bench at a show. If the dog is taken where sheep have

been, there is the chance that it can have a tick or two sucking blood. On no account pull the tick out with tweezers, the head of the tick will be left embedded in the skin of the dog. We spray the dog with Nuvutop, obtained from the vet, and also treat the bench and bedding. We do this after a walk and when we bring the dog home from a show. Keep a close check when you are grooming, this is the best time to spot those tell-tale signs of infestation. During the summer months grass seeds might become embedded in the dog's eyes or between the toes. A quick check when the dog is brought home will save a lot of trouble later on and may well save on vet's bills.

CHAPTER NINETEEN

Rescue Schemes

THE dedicated ladies who cope with the large number of unwanted working sheepdogs and border collies are to be congratulated on their dedication. Mrs Hazel Monk and her helpers mainly cater for the Border Collie Club of Great Britain and Val Ricketts works with the Southern Border Collie Club. It is a marathon task because most dogs in need of new homes are working sheepdogs that have been sold with the name of border collie, but have no identification papers and so cannot legally be called border collies in the eyes of the Kennel Club.

At first, there was no one person who could take on the work involved in setting up a rescue scheme. We received three or four calls a day from the owners of working sheepdogs who wished to get rid of their wild unruly, unsuitable house pets. They had seen the border collie working sheep on television, in the programme 'One Man and his Dog' and without sensible assessment they had gone to the nearest pet shop, puppy farm or department store and bought a black and white puppy. With no recommendation or advice from the sales person, they had bought the puppy home – and then the trouble had started. The dog found itself cooped up in a town environment, sometimes living in a small flat, with owners who were completely unaware of the training that was needed. Then, when the puppy matured, it behaved as it was bred to behave, full of life and extremely active. Finding no outlet for its exuberance, the dog would become neurotic and sometimes vicious. Then the owners would deliver an ultimatum. The dog had to go, but where? The owner did not care, so long as it was found another home. So the dogs and bitches that had turned vicious and had started biting with frustration were offered to other homes, regardless of the consequences. It pained me greatly to refuse help. But the only recourse when the matter had reached that stage was to suggest that the dog was taken to the vet's surgery to be put down. Usually, this is just what the worried owner wanted to hear. He simply did not have the courage to make up his own mind. But eventually the flood of unwanted working sheepdogs got so bad that something had to be done. It was significant that whenever possible, these were not Kennel Club registered border collies that needed to be found new homes. In fact, in all the years that I have been involved with the breed I have only had one Kennel Club registered border collie that needed a new home and that was easy to place with a breeder.

The Border Collie Club of Great Britain pioneered the official rescue scheme with Mrs Hazel Monk taking on the unenviable task of finding homes. Hazel and a group of volunteers in the Birmingham area had worked together over several years trying to re-home unwanted strays of all breeds. Hazel then found herself involved in rescuing her favourite breed, the border collie. 'They were mostly un-registered working sheepdogs, but just a few had been registered', she said.

The never ending stream of unwanted collies was too much for her to cope with alone, so other people offered assistance in different parts of England. At first, Hazel would collect an unwanted dog or bitch, but the scale of the operation has made this impossible. Although we must receive as many calls for advice and help as Hazel does, they are never from the owners of Kennel Club registered border collies. So we can only come to the conclusion that it is not these dogs that are finding their way on to the Rescue Scheme. The show people are not breeding indiscriminately and flooding the market with unwanted show dogs and I only hope that it never happens.

We frequently get calls from owners of dogs that have been bought direct from a farmer, who has sold off surplus stock as pets. We suggest that these owners get back in touch with the farmer and ask him to take the dog back. The answer is always the same, 'We have and he doesn't want to know.' There are other owners who suggest that their wild, unruly pet is found a home on a farm, where it can be trained to work sheep. They are most surprised when they are told that as the dog was sold as unwanted surplus stock in the first place, it is very unlikely that the farmer will want it back to train on his prize sheep. This is a very sad situation and one that will only improve when puppy buyers are told what a working sheepdog is and what the name implies. Breeders and sellers must be honest and tell all would be owners what the border collie needs in order to adapt to a new environment.

I was once involved with a complaint that was being investigated under the Trades Description Act. They bought a black and white dog to me and asked for my opinion as to whether it could be described as a pure bred border collie. The owners had been to a local kennels and been sold a black and white dog for £75 and it had been named as a border collie. They had taken it to a training class and one or two people had told them it did not resemble a border collie at all. As a championship show judge, I was called in to examine the dog. Even a novice would have been doubtful, but I had to give a detailed assessment of its resemblance to another breed, which I stated was a cocker spaniel. Its ears were flat to its head, and although border collies can also have low set ears, these were of cocker spaniel type with curls. The coat texture was completely wrong, its feet were large, in fact too large for its type. The angulation of its rear was wrong and it was very low to ground with too heavy bone for a border collie puppy. The case was taken to court and the kennel owner was fined. Later it was mentioned that this was not the first time that mixed parentage puppies had been sold. When the owners queried if they had a pedigree for the puppy, they were told that border collies were not shown and they did not have Kennel Club papers. This was in 1984 and the owners should have checked on the breed before getting involved in buying one.

The show border collie has to be of good temperament, steady and intelligent, and has, of necessity, to be more domesticated than its counterpart that works on the farms. It cannot nip the judge or chase the other dogs around the ring, it must be trained in a different way to use its intelligence and accept the situation that confronts it. When a person buys a border collie for show, it will not look any different from most of the other dogs, it might be a little more domesticated, and not so hyperactive. This is the dog that will adjust quite happily to the show world and with such an intelligent animal it will not take too much effort. This transition to a calmer temperament is becoming increasingly apparent and there are now a number of good looking borders that have been bred solely for the the show ring.

Names and Contact numbers

Mrs Hazel Monk, Birmingham   Telephone 021 430 3899
Mrs Val Ricketts, Worthing   Telephone 0903 63522.

Appendices

CHALLENGE CERTIFICATES
* Denotes Breed Specialist
(Up to and including Border Union 1988)

Sh.Ch Tilehouse Cassius at Beagold
Awarded by:
Mrs C. Sutton
Mrs M. Gascoigne★
Mr W. Finlay★
Mrs I. Combe★

Sh.Ch Tracelyn Gal
Awarded by:
Mrs C. Sutton
Mrs M. Gascoigne★
Mrs V. Yates
Mrs M. Hopkinson★

Sch.Ch Asoka Navajho of Firelynx
Awarded by:
Mr W. Dixon★
Mr D. Samuel
Mrs P. Green
Mr W. Finlay★

Sh.Ch Muirend Border Dream
Awarded by:
Mr W. Dixon★
Mrs M. Gascoigne★
Mr W. Finlay★
Mr D. Samuel
Mrs Sydenham-Clarke
Mr W. Finlay★

Tracelyn Saul
Awarded by:
Mrs A. Arch

Merrybrook Apache
Awarded by:
Mrs A. Arch

Sh.Ch Tork of Whenway
Awarded by:
Mrs M. Leigh★
Mrs J. Collis★
Mrs C. Sutton
Mr W. Dixon★
Mrs K. Holliday★

Sh.Ch Welsh Queen Bess
Awarded by:
Mrs M. Leigh★
Mr W. Finlay★
Mrs A. Arch

Sh.Ch Mizanne The Witch
Awarded by:
Mrs J. Collis★
Mrs C.Sutton
Mrs M. Gascoigne★
Mrs M. Evans★
Dr A. Leigh★

Sh.Ch Melodor Flint at Dykebar
Awarded by:
Mrs M. Gascoigne★
Mrs V. Yates
Mr D. Samuel
Mrs M. Boggia
Mr W. Finlay★
Mr A. Ashley-Roberts★
Mr W. Dixon★
Miss K. Lister★
Mr J. Bispham

Sh.Ch. Kathmick Griff
Awarded by:
Mrs I. Combe★
Mrs A. Arch
Mrs J. Collis★
Mrs P. Green
Mrs M. Boggia

Sh.Ch Whenway Janita of Monkfield
Awarded by:
Mrs I. Combe★
Mrs M. Gascoigne★
Mrs M. Boggia
Mrs G. Broadley
Mrs B. Beaumont★

Vickyian Queen Guinevere
Awarded by:
Mrs N. Simpson★
Dr A. Leigh★

Sh.Ch
Viber Travelling Matt from
Corinlea
Awarded by:
Mr R. Henry★
Mrs D. Lewin★
Miss M. Lucas★
Mrs P. Walsh★
Mr R. Walsh★
Mrs N. Simpson★
Mrs S. A. Kilsby★
Mr E. Broadhurst★
Mrs P. McAdam
Mrs I. Combe★

Altricia Kelly of Chartop
Awarded by:
Mrs K. Lister★
Mrs P. McAdam

Sh.Ch
Snowmere Tweed
Awarded by:
Mrs P. Walsh★
Mrs A. Arch
Mrs B. Beaumont★
Mr R. James

Shipelle Blossom
Awarded by:
Mr B. Kilsby★

Sh.Ch
Fieldbank Merry Meg
Awarded by:
Mrs A. Arch
Mr T. Horner
Mr W. Dixon★

Mizanne The Joker
Awarded by:
Mrs. I Combe★

Corinlea Fleet
Awarded by:
Mr J. Gascoigne★

Muirend Border Bounty
Awarded by:
Mr W. Dixon★

Rosehurst The George
Awarded by:
Mrs M. Collier★
Mrs A. McDonald

Sh.Ch
Passims Bonnie at Beagold
Awarded by:
Mrs B. Beaumont★
Mr R. Searle
Dr B. Raven
Mrs M. Boggia

Sh.Ch
Fieldbank Professional
Awarded by:
Mrs M. Evans★
Mrs D. Lewin★
Mrs B. Beaumont★
Mr A. Ashley-Roberts★
Mrs A. Amos★

Nell of Tracelyn
Awarded by:
Mr T. Holliday★

Viber Gypsy Lace
Awarded by:
Mr D. Samuel

Fieldbank Midnight
Melody
Awarded by:
Mr R. James

Sh.Ch
Lethans Hopeful Flame
Awarded by:
Mrs M. Gascoigne★
Mrs M. Hopkinson★
Mr R. Searle
Mrs M. Collier★
Mr W. Finlay★

Viber Aiming High at
Mobella
Awarded by:
Mrs D. Lewin★

Sh.Ch
Melodor Flurry at
Falconmoor
Awarded by:
Mrs M. Evans★
Mr W. Dixon★
Mrs V. Yates
Mr D. Samuel
Mr A. Ashley-Roberts★
Mr W. Dixon★

Tracelyn Shepherd Boy
Awarded by:
Mrs V. Yates

Sh.Ch
Muirend Border Blessing
Awarded by:
Mrs J. Collis★
Mr J. Kirk
Mrs D. Hollis

Coteroyde Beau Ideal
Awarded by:
Mr J. Braddon

Mizanne The Whisky
Awarded by:
Mr R. Walsh★

Detania Kelly
Awarded by:
Mr J. Braddon

Obed. Ch. Whenway Mist
of Wizaland
Awarded by:
Grp.Ct. Sutton

Mobella Country of
Santramore
Awarded by:
Mr B. James

Redrobs Cassie
Awarded by:
Mrs M. Evans★
Mrs C. Coxall

Beagold Sugar Ray
Awarded by:
Mrs D. Hollis

Cluff of Mobella
Awarded by:
Mr T. Holliday★

Wizaland McIntosh
Awarded by:
Mr R. Henry★

Avocks Ellie
Awarded by:
Mrs A. Arch

Sh.Ch
Muirend Border Gypsy
Awarded by:
Mr D. Samuel
Mrs P. Walsh★
Mrs J. Collis★

Colthurst Ruby Red
Awarded by:
Mrs S. A. Kilsby★

Wizaland Jake of Eyot
Awarded by:
Mrs T. Taylor★
Dr A. Leigh★

Ruscombe Astra
Awarded by:
Mrs I. Combe★

Sh.Ch.
Mizanne The Lady Lucinda
Awarded by:
Mrs M. Boggia
Mr F. Cosme★
Mrs M. Hopkinson★

Sh.Ch
Melodor Robbie
Awarded by:
Mrs Sydenham-Clarke
Mrs N. Simpson★
Mrs A. Arch
Mrs P. Green

Sh.Ch
Huntroyde Beau Brummel
at Sanrian
Awarded by:
Mrs M. Hopkinson★
Mrs M. Boggia
Mrs J. Collis★
Mr S. Pascoe

Detania Zara
Awarded by:
Mr K. Bullock
Mrs T. Taylor★

Sh.Ch
Merrybrook Lisa
Awarded by:
Mrs M. Boggia
Mr A. Ashley-Roberts★
Mrs M. Collier★
Mr R. Henry★

Sh.Ch
Whenway Rhys of Mizanne
Awarded by:
Mrs M. Gascoigne★
Mrs B. Beaumont★
Mrs K. Holliday★

Whenway Lara
Awarded by:
Mrs B. Beaumont★
Mr K. Bullock

Sh.Ch
Beagold Louis
Awarded by:
Mr J. Kirk
Mrs C. Sutton
Mr K. Bullock
Mr T. Horner
Mrs M. Evans★
Mr B. Kilsby★
Mr D. Samuel

Sh.Ch
Tilehouse Tipp
Awarded by:
Mrs G. Broadley
Mr D. Samuel
Mrs J. Collis★

Sh.Ch
Shace Merry Megan
Awarded by:
Mr W. Finlay★
Mrs I. Combe★
Mr J. Gascoigne★
Mrs A. Arch
Mrs M. Collier★

Tracelyn Mandy of
Melodor
Awarded by:
Mrs C. Sutton
Mrs P. Green

Corinlea Flurry
Awarded by:
Mrs P. Walsh★
Mr J. Bispham

Robert The Sweep
Awarded by:
Mrs C. Coxall

Allado The Real McCoy
Awarded by:
Dr B. Raven

Sh.Ch
Rosehurst Twilight Crystal
Awarded by:
Mrs P. Green
Mr J. Gascoigne★
Mrs N. Simpson★
Mrs K. Holliday★
Mrs M. Gascoigne★

Sh.Ch
Huntroyde Black Shadow
of Ettaswell
Awarded by:
Mr K. Bullock
Dr A. Leigh★
Mr R. James

Sh.Ch
Corinlea Rona
Awarded by:
Mr B. Kilsby★
Mrs J. Collis★
Miss K. Lister★

Sh.Ch
Muirend Border Maid
Awarded by:
Mr R. James
Mr S. Pascoe
Mr E. Broadhurst★

Altricia Kev
Awarded by:
Miss F. Hamilton
Mrs M. Gascoigne★

Caristan Forever Amber
Awarded by:
Mrs M. Gascoigne★

Black Lace of Shipelle
Awarded by:
Mr R. James

Sh.Ch
Whenway Hope of Corinlea
Awarded by:
Mrs M. Gascoigne★
Mrs M. Evans★
Mr J. Gascoigne★

Sacul Highland Mist from
Corinlea
Awarded by:
Miss M. Lucas★
Mrs K. Holliday★

Sh.Ch
Wizaland Jake of Eyot
Awarded by:
Mrs J. Collis★
Miss T. Taylor
Dr A. Leigh

Tomozine Celtic Maiden
Awarded by:
Miss F. Hamilton

Detania Jack Tar
Awarded by:
Mrs M. Boggia

Crufts winners given challenge certificates from 1982 onwards

DOGS

1982   Sh.Ch. Tilehouse Cassius at Beagold (Brocken Sweep of Tilehouse x Fly of
        Tilehouse)
1983   Sh.Ch. Tork of Whenway (Clun Roy I x Belle)
1984   Sh.Ch. Tork of Whenway (Clun Roy I x Belle)
1985   Sh.Ch. Huntroyde Beau Brummel at Sanrian (Cliff x Huntroyde Bonny Bess)
1986   Sh.Ch. Melodor Robbie (Muirend Border Reiver x Muirend Border Ballad of
        Melodor)
1987   Lethans Hopeful Flame (Kirkfield Kirk x Kirkfield Shell) Now a Show
        Champion
1988   Sh.Ch.Lethans Hopeful Flame (Kirkfield Kirk x Kirkfield Shell)

BITCHES

1982   Sh.Ch. Muirend Border Dream (Pioneer of Muirend x Nimble of Muirend)
1983   Sh.Ch. Mizanne the Witch (Asoka Apache of Firelynx x Cass of Mizanne)
1984   Sh.Ch. Melodor Flurry at Falconmoor (Muirend Border Reiver x Muirend
        Border Ballad of Melodor)
1985   Sh.Ch. Tracelyn Gal (Cymro x Jill)
1986   Sh.Ch. Fieldbank Merry Meg (Glen x Fly)
1987   Sh.Ch. Rosehurst Twilight Crystal (Sh.Ch Tork of Whenway x Sh.Ch.
        Tracelyn Gal)
1988   Sh.Ch. Muirend Border Dream

List of Firsts

First Club	The Border Collie Club of Great Britain
First Show	The Border Collie Club of Great Britain Open Show with Obedience
First Club in the South	The Southern Border Collie Club
First BIS at Ch. Show	Mr John Ritchie's Sh.Ch. Melodor Flint at Dykebar
First Branch	East Anglian Branch of the Border Collie Club of GB
First to be invited to the Contest of Champions	Sh.Ch. Tilehouse Cassius at Beagold
First CC winner dog	Sh.Ch. Tilehouse Cassius at Beagold Crufts 1982
First CC winner bitch	Sh.Ch. Tracelyn Gal. Crufts 1982
First Sh.Ch. dog	Sh.Ch. Tilehouse Cassius at Beagold
First Sh.Ch. bitch	Sh.Ch. Muirend Border Dream
First prick eared dog to win CC	Whenway Hope of Corinlea (Sh.Ch.)
First prick eared bitch to win CC	Mizanne the Witch (Sh.Ch.)
First Tri coloured dog to win CC	Sh.Ch. Kathmick Griff
First Tri coloured bitch to win CC	Sh.Ch. Tracelyn Gal
First All round judge to give CCs	Mrs Catherine Sutton Crufts 1982
First Specialist judge to give CCs at Crufts	Mrs Joyce Collis 1983
First Junior warrent winner Dog	Echofell in Wisaland
First Junior warrent winner Bitch	Sh.Ch. Muirend Border Dream
First Res. Group winner D.	Sh.Ch. Tilehouse Cassius at Beagold. Welsh KC Ch. Show 1981
First Res. Group winner B	Sh.Ch. Melodor Flurry at Falconmoor
First Home Bred Ch. d.	Sh.Ch. Melodor Robbie
First Home bred Ch. b.	Muirend Border Dream
First Veteran CC winner Dog	Sh.Ch. Tilehouse Cassius at Beagold
First Veteran CC winner bitch	Merrybrook Apache
First Ch. Show	The Border Collie Club of GB (for the breed)
First Ch. Show Judges	Mr Tom Horner and Mr Bill Dixon (for the breed)
First Red Merle CC winner	Colhurst Ruby Red
First Red/white CC winner	Sh.Ch. Passims Bonnie at Beagold
First Red/white dog to win CC	
First Red/white bitch	Sh.Ch. Passims Bonnie at Beagold
First Top Border Collie winner for the year	Sh.Ch. Asoka Navajho of Firelynx. 1978

First Dog to win CC and BOB at Crufts two years running. Res. CC the third year. Sh. Ch. Tork of Whenway.

SHOW CHAMPIONS
(To Border Union 1988)

Name	Sex	No of cc's	Age at Title (months)	Sire	Dam	Owner	Breeder
1. Tilehouse Cassius at Beagold	Male	4	47	Brocken Sweep of Tilehouse	Fly of Tilehouse	Mrs Collis/Mr Cosme	Iris Combe
2. Muirend Border Dream	Female	6	33	Pioneer of Muirend	Nimble of Muirend	Nan Simpson	Owner
3. Asoka Navajho of Firelynx	Male	4	74	Shep (ISDS)	Asoka Cloud	Mr & Mrs Miller	Peggy Litton
4. Tork of Whenway	Male	5	37	Clun Roy I (ISDS)	Belle (ISDS)	Mr & Mrs Kilsby	Mr Baylis
5. Tracelyn Gal	Female	4	43	Cymro (ISDS)	Gill (ISDS)	Mr & Mrs Broadhurst	Mr J. Ritchie
6. Welsh Queen Bess	Female	3	65	Tweed (ISDS)	Nan (ISDS)	Mr & Mrs Mitchell	Mr D. Williams
7. Melodor Flurry at Falconmoor	Female	6	31	Muirend Border Reiver	Muirend Border Ballad	Mesdames Haydock & Croft	Chris McLean
8. Kathmick Griff	Male	5	64	Langloch Len (ISDS)	Jess (ISDS)	Mrs Gascoigne	Mr Hope
9. Melodor Flint at Dykebar	Male	9	33	Muirend Border Reiver	Muirend Border Ballad	Mr J. Ritchie	Chris McLean
10. Whenway Janita of Monkfield	Female	5	46	Sh.Ch. Asoka Navajho of Firelynx	Wisp from Whenway	Mrs H. Monk	Mr & Mrs Kilsby
11. Mizanne The Witch	Female	5	71	Asoka Apache of Firelynx	Cass of Mizanne	Mr & Mrs Lewin	Owners
12. Huntroyde Black Shadow of Ettaswell	Male	3	46	Cliff (ISDS)	Huntroyde Bonny Bess	Mr & Mrs Henry	Mrs K. West
13. Whenway Hope of Corinlea	Male	3	45	Sh.Ch. Tork of Whenway	Dana of Tracelyn	Mr & Mrs Holiday	Mr & Mrs Kilsby
14. Rosehurst Twilight Crystal	Female	5	20	Sh.Ch. Tork of Whenway	Sh.Ch. Tracelyn Gal	Mr & Mrs Broadhurst	Owners
15. Melodor Robbie	Male	4	60	Muirend Border Reiver	Muirend Border Ballad	Mrs C. McLean	Owner
16. Beagold Louis	Male	7	29	Sh.Ch. Tilehouse Cassius of Beagold	Bonnie of Beagold	Mrs Collis/Mr Cosme	Owners
17. Tilehouse Tipp	Male	3	57	Tilehouse Topper	Fly of Tilehouse	Mr & Mrs Green	Iris Combe
18. Fieldbank Professional	Male	5	81	Shanvaal Glen	Lady Fleck of Fieldbank	Miss K. Lister	Owner
19. Fieldbank Merry Meg	Female	3	51	Glen (ISDS)	Fly (ISDS)	Miss K. Lister	Mr Fouracre
20. Muirend Border Blessing	Female	3	42	Tweed of Muirend	Sh.Ch. Muirend Border Dream	Mrs N. Simpson	Owner
21. Merrybrook Lisa	Female	4	25	Sh.Ch. Melodor Flint at Dykebar	Merrybrook Sarah	Mr & Mrs Hoare	Owners
22. Shace Merry Megan	Female	5	30	Skip (ISDS)	Fly (ISDS)	Mr & Mrs Durward	Mr J. Morgan
23. Corinlea Rona	Female	3	40	Firelynx Chiri Gvano of Corinlea	Whenway Gypsy at Corinlea	Mr & Mrs Holliday	Owners
24. Huntroyde Beau Brummel at Sanrian	Male	4	59	Cliff (ISDS)	Huntroyde Bonny Bess	Mr & Mrs Goddard	Mrs K. West
25. Muirend Border Gypsy	Female	3	71	Bill (ISDS)	Sh.Ch. Muirend Border Dream	Mr & Mrs Holliday	Mrs N. Simpson
26. Snowmere Tweed	Male	4	72	Gemond Castor	Megan of Snowmere	Miss J. Mockford	Owner
27. Viber Travelling Matt from Corinlea	Male	10	21	Cluff of Mobella	Sacul Highland Mist from Corinlea	Mr & Mrs Holliday	Mr & Mrs Gray
28. Whenway Rhys of Mizanne	Male	3	82	Sh.Ch. Asoka Navajho of Firelynx	Wisp from Whenway	Mr & Mrs Lewin	Mr & Mrs Kilsby
29. Mizanne The Lady Lucinda	Female	3	46	Sh.Ch. Kathmick Griff	Sh.Ch. Mizanne The Witch	Miss T. Mills	Mr & Mrs Lewin
30. Lethans Hopeful Flame	Male	5	62	Kirkfield Kirk	Kirkfield Shell	Mrs J. Hastie	Owner
31. Muirend Border Maid	Female	3	93	Muirend Border Reiver	Muirend Border Lace	Mr & Mrs Bromwich	Mrs N. Simpson
32. Passims Bonnie at Beagold	Female	4	28	Sh.Ch. Whenway Rhys of Mizanne	Cotesbelle Kirsty at Passim	Mrs Collis/Mr Cosme	Miss S. Ader
33. Wizaland Jake of Eyot	Male	3	43	Sh.Ch. Tork of Whenway	Ob.Ch. Whenway Hut of Wizaland	Mrs P. Haydock	Mrs S. Large

Kennel Club Registrations 1976–1987

1976	–	5
1977	–	212
1978	–	368
1979	–	843
1980	–	735
1981	–	718
1982	–	756
1983	–	768
1984	–	968
1985	–	1052
1986	–	1131
1987	–	917

Border Collies were recognised by the Kennel Club to be included in the Show Register in 1976. They were originally from the International Sheepdog Society Register and this was reflected in the small numbers. In 1977 there was a large jump in registrations and this upward trend has continued.